Selling on the
Internet

D1538083

Other Books by James Gonyea

On-Line Job Search Companion: A Complete Guide to Hundreds of Career Planning and Job-Hunting Resources Available via Your Computer

Career Selector 2001

Working for America

Selling on the Internet

How to Open an Electronic Storefront and Have Millions of Customers Come to You!

James C. Gonyea

Wayne M. Gonyea

McGraw-Hill

New York   San Francisco   Washington, D.C.   Auckland   Bogotá
Caracas   Lisbon   London   Madrid   Mexico City   Milan
Montreal   New Delhi   San Juan   Singapore
Sydney   Tokyo   Toronto

Library of Congress Cataloging-in-Publication Data

Gonyea, James C.
    Selling on the Internet : how to open an electronic storefront and
have millions of customers come to you! / James C. Gonyea, Wayne M.
Gonyea.
     p.   cm.
    Includes index.
    ISBN 0-07-024187-2 (pbk./disk)
    1. Business enterprises—United States—Computer networks.
2. Internet advertising—United States.   3. Internet marketing—
United States.   4. Internet (Computer network)   5. World Wide Web
(Information retrieval system.)   I. Gonyea, Wayne M.   II. Title.
HD30.37.G66   1996
658.8′4—dc20   96-4217
                                                            CIP

1 2 3 4 5 6 7 8 9 0 DOC/DOC 9 0 1 0 9 8 7 6

"To Market, To Market ..." was written by Rob Kost. Mr. Kost works for PRODIGY Services Company in its Internet Development Group, and may be reached via e-mail at *kost@PRODIGY.com*. The views expressed in this chapter are those of Mr. Kost, and do not necessarily represent those of PRODIGY Services Company.

"Legal Considerations" was written by the late Attorney Edward Frankel. Mr. Frankel was Director of Global Innovations Group.

The data used to produce **"Internet Access Service Providers"** was drawn from the InterNIC Leased Line Providers list published via the Internet by InterNIC, a project of the National Science Foundation, and is reprinted here with permission. © Copyright General Atomics. All rights reserved.

"Netiquette" was written by Arlene Rinaldi, Senior Computer Programmer/Analyst at Florida Atlantic University. Ms. Rinaldi may be reached via e-mail at *rinaldi@acc.fau.edu*.

NetCruiser program is copyrighted © 1994 by NetCom.

P/N 024293-3
Part of
ISBN 0-07-024187-2

The sponsoring editor for this book was Betsy Brown, the editing supervisor was Fred Dahl, and the production supervisor was Suzanne Rapcavage. It was set in Palatino by Inkwell Publishing Services.

Printed and bound by R. R. Donnelley & Sons Company.

This book is printed on recycled, acid-free paper containing a minimum of 50 percent recycled de-inked fiber.

In memory of
Edward Frankel
Attorney at Law
A good friend and a trusted legal advisor. Your voice may be still, but I
can still hear your words of wisdom.

To my fellow entrepreneurs who each day do battle to make their
enterprise a success. In a world where business is global and moves at
the speed of light, I offer this guide as a new resource with which you
can more easily transform your dreams into reality.
And, as before and always, to Pam and Korie.

James C. Gonyea

To Leslie, Tony, Lisa, and Mike for a never ending well of
encouragement, love, and support. Especially to Kassie for making the
world a better place.

Wayne M. Gonyea

Contents

4. To Market, to Market ...   **79**

How to market and advertise your storefront on the Internet
to attract customers to your electronic place of business.

5. Selling Overseas   **95**

Special considerations when you're selling products and
services abroad.

6. Legal Considerations   101

Learn how to protect your business data, products, and services that you market online, as well as what legal rights your customers have when it comes to using your intellectual property, products, and services.

7. Security Issues   123

*How to protect sensitive data, such as credit card
information and your confidential business files, from
prying eyes on the Internet.*

8. Actual Storefronts in Use Today   131

*Actual screen shots from the home pages of some of
America's leading electronic storefronts. See for yourself
how business is capitalizing on the use of the Internet.*

Preface

It's not everyday that you can witness a technological revolution. But that's exactly what's happening today in the field of telecommunications—a global revolution driven by the development and use of high-speed computers and computer online networks. Certainly, we are all aware that voice communication around the world has been a reality for most of this century. However, now, in only a matter of seconds, data, text, photos, video, sound, and graphics can also be transmitted at the speed of light from one computer to any other computer located anywhere on the planet.

While such instant communication is changing forever how individuals interact with each other across political, cultural, economic, and geographical borders, its impact on how average business leaders and entrepreneurs can now conduct business worldwide is nothing short of revolutionary. The global marketplace is finally here!

At the very heart of this technological phenomenon is the Internet, often referred to as the *Information Superhighway*—millions of computers linked worldwide via phone lines and cables carrying information from person to person at the blink of an eye. Viewed on your computer screen, the Internet offers users various ways of "interacting" or "interfacing" with each other, from basic text displays where only the printed word is visible to elaborate graphical, multimedia displays that include the use of text, sound, graphics, photos, and live video. Through the use of these graphical displays, commonly referred to as *electronic storefronts*, business leaders, both large and small, are "setting up shop" on the Internet, and from such locations are selling an unlimited variety of products and services worldwide. And so can you!

Using the Internet, people from all corners of the globe are redefining how the age-old processes of buying and selling products and services between shop owners and customers is transacted. Merchants located in Tampa, Tokyo, or anywhere on the planet for that matter can now market their products and services instantly via electronic storefronts to customers who themselves are located anywhere in the world—without the two parties physically facing each other.

Selling on the Internet is your guide to learning how you, as a business person or entrepreneur, can harness the power of the Internet and through the use of electronic storefronts expand your business worldwide.

Like the great industrial revolution of the nineteenth century, today's leading edge technology, producing what historians are already calling the "information age," is bringing about profound changes in how we live and conduct business. And like all revolutions, some will prosper from the change and others will be little affected, while—worse—still others will become victims of the new guard. *Selling on the Internet* can help you avoid the pitfalls inherent in using the Internet to ensure that your chances of success are good.

While the revolution is in full swing, it's also still in its infancy, primarily because the technology underlying the development of the Internet and the use of electronic storefronts is constantly evolving, changing, improving, and advancing. The promise of what is to come is for many individuals very exciting, only somewhat predictable, and largely unknown.

With *Selling on the Internet*, you have a front row seat to watch the revolution unfold from the safety of your desktop or laptop computer. If you wish, you may also join in on the action, open up your own electronic storefront, learn how to succeed online, and become part of the force that will shape the future of the Internet, especially how commerce is and will be conducted.

 Selling on the Internet comes bundled with a complimentary copy of *NetCruiser*, a Windows-based, leading-edge software program from Net-Com that provides you with full access to the Internet, including a powerful web browser program to access any of the many electronic storefronts already open for business.

Recent AT&T television commercials foretell of a world where live video, voice, and data communications will be transmitted, for business or personal use, from any one location on the planet to any other location without the need for ground-based phone lines. Well, guess what? Instant person-to-person communications is already here and more of this technology is on its way. If a giant telecommunications company like AT&T is predicting the coming of such technological marvels, then you can be sure that even more marvelous things are in development and coming soon!

For entrepreneurs who thrive on the edge and embrace today's leading technology, pushing it to its limits to see where it can lead and what positive effect it can have on business, the Internet can be a dream come true and offer the promise of new found riches. The next promising frontier is the vast and uncharted "lands" of cyberspace—the online world encountered as you travel down the Information Superhighway.

Selling on the Internet is your guide to how you can successfully conduct business online and prosper from the revolution, how you can set up an electronic storefront on the Information Superhighway from which you can sell your products and services worldwide, and how you can harness the power of your computer to increase the future success of your business.

> *This book is written primarily for individuals engaged in business and other entrepreneurs who have no, or only a marginal, understanding of the Internet and/or electronic storefronts, and who wish to begin to understand the opportunities that are available using these technological marvels.*

As a result of reading this book, you should be able to develop a basic understanding of the Internet and the value of electronic storefronts, be able to converse intelligently on the subject, find actual storefronts online, identify storefront developers, understand what equipment and information is necessary to set up a storefront, and learn how to manage a storefront on a daily basis.

As early pioneers ourselves with storefronts dating back to 1989, we have witnessed first-hand the benefits of setting up shop online, and we have learned a few things regarding how to manage a profitable storefront. Also, as professional career, employment, and business counselors and consultants by trade, dedicated to helping individuals achieve a higher level of success, we are pleased to share with you what we have learned, in the hope that our insight will help you better achieve your business goals and objectives.

Comments from readers regarding this book, especially suggestions for the next edition, should be directed to:

Gonyea and Associates, Inc.
1151 Maravista Drive
New Port Richey, FL 34655

James C. Gonyea
Wayne M. Gonyea

Acknowledgments

Few books on the subject of the Internet can be written by one or two authors nowadays; the subject matter is simply too vast and constantly changing and evolving. This book would not have been completed as quickly and as well without the assistance of the following individuals. We deeply appreciate their assistance.

To *Rob Kost*, one of today's hottest stars in the field of computer online services, we owe a special vote of thanks for helping us understand the unique marketing opportunities and demands awaiting those entrepreneurs who conduct business on the Internet. Rob's leadership can help us all avoid the road hazards that lurk on the Information Superhighway.

To *Steven Connors* and *Alan Stiavetti* at NetCom for their generous support and for allowing us to provide our readers with a complimentary copy of NetCruiser, with which the marvels of the Internet can be fully accessed. It's one thing to write about the Internet, yet another to actually travel it, and NetCruiser is a great vehicle with which to witness the Internet first hand.

To the late attorney *Edward Frankel*, of Global Innovations Group, whose friendship and legal advice have always helped us steer the proper course for our business ventures. We deeply appreciate his insights regarding the legal rights of storefront owners and customers. We will miss his friendship and counsel.

To *Mark Tolman* of InterConnect West for his assistance in helping us understand the cost realities of developing a direct link to the Internet, as well as for his general guidance regarding the development of storefront services.

To *Heidi Kongieser* and *Jenn Anderson* for creating many of the graphic illustrations found in this book.

To *Arlene H. Rinaldi* at Florida Atlantic University for her unique insight and contribution to the examination of Netiquette rules—behavior that we all should adopt if the Internet is to remain a warm and welcome highway.

To *Paul Wilson* at InterNIC who graciously allowed us to use their extensive list of Internet Access Service Providers. Your assistance is much appreciated.

To *Don Wood*, who manned the phones, typed the ads, and otherwise freed us from the daily chores of running our businesses to enable us to have the time necessary to write this book. OK, now let's play golf!

To *Kevin Machos* for his assistance in compiling the Internet Glossary.

To *James Getty* of Royal Books for his assistance in compiling information for the Internet Resource Directory.

To *Kurt Stammberger* at RSA Data Security, Inc. for helping us understand how encryption technology can make the Internet a safe and secure place for conducting business.

To the many, many individuals who graciously shared with us their storefront experiences and testimonials. The time you shared with us was most enlighting and deeply appreciated.

And, of course, to *Betsy Brown* at McGraw-Hill for her assistance in shaping the early content of this book, for her guidance throughout its development, and for her continued support of our literary ideas over the years.

Selling on the
Internet

1

Welcome to the Internet

Any discussion of electronic storefronts can be accomplished only *after* a basic understanding of the Internet itself has been established. After all, you would never open a new office location along a busy highway without first understanding how you and your customers can best travel the highway to find and visit your location.

This chapter presents a general overview of the Internet, covering such topics as:

❑ What is the Internet?

❑ Why was the Internet created?

❑ Why is the Internet so popular?

❑ Who's using the Internet and for what purpose?

❑ Who owns or controls the Internet?

❑ How can one access the Internet?

❑ How does one travel on the Internet?

Perhaps you already have a solid understanding of the Internet, how it operates, and how it can be accessed, and you are now ready to learn about developing an electronic storefront. If so, you may wish to skip this chapter and move directly to the next chapter entitled, "Electronic Storefronts: The Internet Is Open for Business!"

If you are new to the Internet, then you should read this chapter carefully. Then, if you wish to learn more about the Internet in general, you will find several excellent publications listed in App. C, "Internet Resource Directory."

As you complete the later sections of this chapter, it is highly recommended that you install and begin to use the NetCruiser software program included with this book, to become familiar with the Internet concepts presented in this chapter. Only from actually traveling on the Internet can you fully understand its value and potential to you as a businessperson.

What Is the Internet?

As stated in the Preface, the Internet is a collection of millions of interconnected computers located in countries throughout the world—all linked by phone lines and high-speed cables to form a gigantic computer network system. Actually, the Internet is a collection of thousands of smaller computer networks, each network linked to the next network to form one large worldwide network.

To illustrate how the Internet operates, assume a company called Glendale Socks located in London, England owned ten computers, all of which were located on various floors of its five-story office building in London. These computers could be linked together using cables or phone lines to form a *local area network* (referred to as a LAN). As a result, any information stored or created on one computer could be transmitted to (or

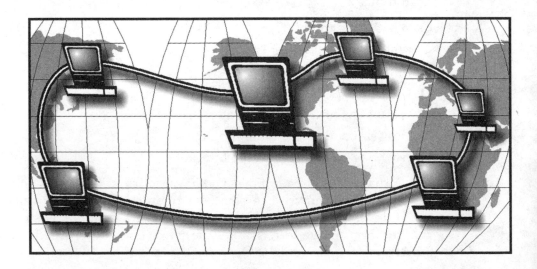

accessed by) any other computer connected to the network. Such an arrangement would certainly save time and effort on the part of the Glendale Sock employees, who could quickly and easily share information without moving physically from floor to floor or from office to office.

Now imagine that Glendale Socks has decided to open a second office, but this time in Cambridge, England, a good distance from London. By connecting all the computers at the Cambridge office, as previously done at the London office, and then by connecting the Cambridge network to the London network using a standard phone line, the computers in both offices could then form an even larger network, called a *wide area network* (WAN). Again, information stored or created on any one computer, regardless of its location, could then be transmitted to (or accessed by) any other computer connected to the larger network.

Further imagine that the Glendale Socks company wanted to connect its network to a network already created by one of its raw material suppliers in Frankfurt, Germany. Again, this could be done using existing phone lines. Now the new network has dozens of computers, all sharing information. Continue this practice of connecting networks, but this time think of the process in terms of millions of individuals, organizations, and companies located around the globe. Now you have a *global wide area network* and a good idea as to what the Internet is all about.

Without question, the Internet is the largest network of computers in the world today. Some experts estimate that over 50 million computers are currently connected to the Internet with thousands of new computers being plugged into it daily.

Over this network, vast amounts of data, text, graphics, sound, voice, and live broadcast video are transmitted from one computer to another, often at the speed of light. The Internet is quickly becoming the preferred means of communication by millions of people worldwide, especially by businesses interested in a fast, global, and inexpensive means of reaching customers. Even the President of the United States has opened an electronic storefront from which he can conduct the business of state worldwide (Fig. 1-1).

Due to its enormous size—currently the largest electronic network through which information, of various sorts, can be distributed worldwide—the Internet is often referred to as the *Information Superhighway*. Actually, the term Information Superhighway refers to the electronic network proposed by the Clinton/Gore administration. The vision held by Clinton and Gore for an Information Superhighway is much more elaborate and technologically advanced than the actual Internet in use today. However, until the day comes when the real Information Superhighway is

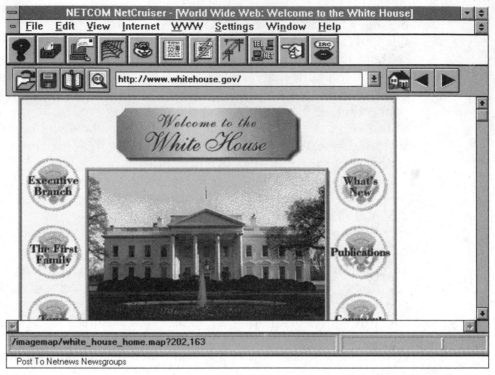

Figure 1-1. The presidential storefront.

paved, the Internet is the next best road we have on which to travel through cyberspace (the territory accessible via the Internet). The Internet is often referred to as the Net, short for Internet.

Why Was the Internet Created?

During the cold war of the 1960s, the United States military establishment, along with many of its university-based research facilities, determined that it needed a secure means of communication among various military facilities and educational research centers around the world. However, considering the political climate of the middle decades of this century, a system was needed that could, in the event of a nuclear attack, remain operational even if sections of the system were destroyed by a direct nuclear bomb hit.

To accomplish this goal, a network of computers was created known as ARPAnet (Advanced Research Projects Agency Network) by the Department of Defense. The network was decentralized, that is, there was no central location from which the entire system could be controlled. In short, the system operated fully independent of any management facility or personnel. Like the electrical wiring system in your home, but only much larger, the ARPAnet was always on, and always ready to transmit information.

Computers were linked together by phone lines and cables, each computer having its own unique address on the ARPAnet system, and special software was written (called TCP/IP) to enable different computer systems to communicate with each other. To ensure that information could be sent securely and accurately from one computer to another, the data was first divided up into short *packets* of information. Each packet represented only a brief section of the full data stream that was intended to be sent from one computer to another, and was encoded with a numerical value representing the exact contents of the packet.

To send information from one computer on the Internet to another, the sending computer would send the first packet to the intended (receiving) computer using the receiving computer's ARPAnet address. Actually the message was sent throughout the entire system. However, only the intended computer with the matching address could actually capture the message for viewing and use by the personnel authorized to use the receiving computer. This was the beauty of the ARPAnet system, if one site was destroyed by a nuclear attack, the other computers would take over and continue to transmit data. As long as your computer was not destroyed, you could send and receive data to and from any other operational computer on the network.

The receiving computer would receive the packet, open it up, determine the numerical value, compare it to the value as encoded within the packet, and then notify the sending computer that the packet was received

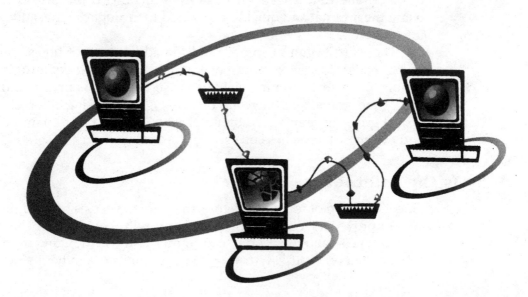

correctly and to send the next packet, or to resend the first packet. Naturally, this was all done at a very fast rate; the transmission of data looked natural and seamless, often taking only seconds to complete.

Special machines, called *gateways*, positioned along the ARPAnet network interpreted data received from various computers systems into a common language (i.e., TCP/IP), thereby enabling computers of different makes and design to talk with each other.

After leaving the sending computer, the data also encountered a series of machines called *routers*. Routers were installed at the intersections of networks and determined which route (i.e., phone line or cable) the data should be sent along (depending on the traffic on each available line) to most quickly reach its destination. Often many different routes were used by a router between the beginning and end of a single transmission of data. Routers acted as traffic cops regulating the transmission of data on the ARPAnet to avoid traffic jams along the way.

In 1982, the National Science Foundation (NSF) upgraded the concept established by ARPAnet when it developed a communications network (called NSFNET) for researchers and scientists worldwide using a series of five supercomputer centers spread across the United States.

Today, the network pioneered by ARPAnet and NSFNET is referred to as the Internet and is essentially the same network, only much larger in terms of the number of computers and users. Another difference is the fact that better and faster communication software is now in use for easier and more rapid transmission of data. Since much of the military's research projects were conducted at selected college and university research centers, it didn't take the nonresearch arm of the educational community long to determine that its regular business functions could also benefit from using the Internet and quickly connected their departments and personnel into the Net.

The word began to spread, and the advantages of this superfast and global network were soon discovered by private and community organizations of all sorts, commercial businesses, as well as private individuals. Today the military is only one of many groups using the Net, with the fastest growing segment of the Internet comprised of private individuals and commercial business users.

Why Is the Internet So Popular?

Since the dawn of recorded history, the human species has sought out new and improved means of communicating with each other. The ability to express one's thoughts, and to communicate those thoughts from one person to another, especially from one generation to another, is perhaps the

greatest attribute that sets humans above all the other living creatures that inhabit the earth.

From the early days, when humans first learned how to use charcoal to form images on cave walls, to today's use of advanced hi-tech electronic communication devices, such as word processing programs and desktop publishing systems, the need to communicate with each other has been a strong and constant necessity of life. Whether it is for sharing our ideas, shaping the behavior of others, teaching or learning from others, or simply expressing our daily feelings and wants, the desire to share in the human experience is a fundamental need of all human beings.

It is no wonder, then, that any device invented by humans that makes communication faster, easier, and more global will be quickly adopted.

From the comfort of your home or office chair, and with the use of a personal computer connected to the Internet via your phone line, you can now communicate with millions of people around the globe in only a matter of seconds. Unlike the singular system offered by the traditional phone service where only voice can be transmitted, communication on the Internet is rich in colors, filled with attractive graphics, photos, and live video, as well as enhanced with sound. The multimedia software interface programs (such as the NetCruiser program bundled with this book) now in use to travel the Internet make the process of communicating with each other an exciting experience.

For the individual interested only in personal contact with other individuals across town, or on the far side of the globe, the Internet offers the largest communication system ever devised by man. For the corporate executive or home-based entrepreneur intent on conducting business locally or overseas, the Internet is the ultimate twenty-first-century *power tool*. Regardless of the physical size of one's business operation, or the depths of one's financial pockets, anyone can set up an electronic storefront and conduct business worldwide.

Travel the Internet today and you'll find many "mom and pop" shops set up next to the giants of Wall Street. Since all storefront owners must use the same kind of electronic displays, it's often next to impossible to tell the corporate giant storefronts from those created by small entrepreneurs working from their kitchen table (Fig. 1-2). The Internet is a gigantic equalizer when it comes to enabling all business proprietors the opportunity to compete on an equal and level playing field.

Who's Using the Internet and for What Purpose?

To list all the Internet users would be impossible, regardless of the size of this book, simply because tens of millions of people are on the Internet today, and this number grows by the millions each month. However, a sampling of what people are doing on the Net can give you an idea of who's using it today.

❏ Individuals are sending e-mail (electronic mail) messages back and forth to each other containing the same content as would be found if you could peek into the United States Postal Service letters being distributed worldwide today. From announcing the birth of a new baby, to discussing the merits of a corporate acquisition, e-mail is one of the fastest means of communication between any two individuals (short of speaking face-to-face) available from our technology treasure chest today.

❏ Politicians from the local level to the highest branches of the executive administration are posting information about their candidacy, with their ideas and position statements on various subjects to aid their constituents in understanding their political objectives and goals.

❏ NASA is publishing photos of various deep space objects taken by the Hubbell Space Telescope—yours for the taking (i.e., downloading).

❏ Various medical centers are posting information about how they're winning the battle against some of today's most devastating illnesses, for other doctors worldwide to access and incorporate into their own practices.

❏ Colleges and universities are posting electronic versions of their college catalogs to draw the attention of prospective students worldwide.

Figure 1-2. A megacorporation and a gift shop, both on the Internet.

❏ The Louvre museum in Paris, France is posting images of artwork from some of the world's greatest masters, as a means of sharing such treasures with the rest of us who can only dream of traveling to its actual location.

❏ The United States Small Business Administration is posting information regarding the information and services available from the federal government to help small businesses succeed.

❏ Employers worldwide are posting help wanted ads for job seekers wishing to secure new employment, and job seekers are posting their resumés worldwide to market their skills.

❏ Various news services—some local and others national or global—are posting wire stories almost as they occur, certainly long before they appear on television or in print.

❏ Support groups of all kinds—from feminists, gay rights advocates, alcoholic anonymous members, motorcycle groupies, parents of troubled teenagers (the list goes on and on)—share information, guidance, and assistance to foster their shared objectives.

❏ Animal lovers and professional animal scientists and veterinarians share their thoughts on the best ways to care for man's best friends.

❏ Many travelers access distant lands worldwide to actually see what's available there, before planning their next get-a-way.

❏ Some of today's hottest musicians and singers share information about themselves, and song clips of their actual work for downloading by fans worldwide.

❏ Thousands of people daily download copies of freeware and shareware software programs to try them out before paying for the complete package, or to share in the wealth of inexpensive and no-cost software available on the Net.

❏ Some of the best movie, theatrical, and book reviews are available to help you find today's best entertainers, artists, and literary giants, as well as up-and-coming new talent.

❑ Financial investors use the Internet to trade stocks and bonds, and to keep track of their investment portfolios.

❑ Busy homemakers can download recipes from all corners of the globe to prepare dishes fit for royalty.

❑ Researchers and scientists from around the globe use the Internet to shorten the development time required to bring about new advances in medicine and science.

❑ Professionals from all disciplines, from accountants to zoologists, use the Internet to share information and services about their professions, and to assist each other in accomplishing shared career endeavors.

❑ And, of course, business entrepreneurs of all kinds, from the large corporate giants to the small "mom and pop" shops, from all countries near and far, are using the Internet to open electronic storefronts, from where they can conduct business.

And so can you!

If you have concluded that just about anybody can use the Internet for some reason or another, then you've got the picture. And remember, the use of the Internet is growing at a phenomenal rate each day: What it is today will not be what it is tomorrow.

Who Owns or Controls the Internet?

No individual, organization, or company owns or manages the Internet. It's not like the commercial computer networks available today, such as America Online, Apple e-World, CompuServe, GEnie, or PRODIGY, where someone owns the service and sets the rules and fees for its use. The Internet belongs to all the individuals who participate in its use, and it is controlled by the very people who use it. Some commonly accepted rules for using the Net have been developed over time by the people who use the Net (see Chap. 11, "Netiquette Guide"), and "penalties" for those who break the rules.

Because no central control system is in place to manage the behavior of the people who use the Net, it can at times become a wild and adventurous place, with some folks actually using the Net for unethical or illegal purposes. The American right to free speech is alive and well on the Net and carefully guarded; so there are places and information available on the Net that may be offensive to certain individuals. However, overall, the information available on the Net is of the kind suitable for all family members.

That being said, you can manage certain behavior that gets far out of line. For example, if you grossly break any of the major Netiquette rules, you could find your computer filled with angry e-mail messages (a practice called *flaming*) from those people of the Internet who take issue with your behavior. Enough e-mail messages can be sent to an individual computer that they can actually cause the receiving computer to malfunction or fail to operate properly.

Before you start using the Internet, especially for business use, please read and follow the guidelines as outlined in the "Netiquette Guide." The Internet is as good a place to travel and work; so let's not destroy a good thing!

How Can One Access the Internet?

For all practical purposes, there are two ways to access the Internet: directly and indirectly. These options are true regardless of whether you wish to access the Internet for the purpose of, for example, only sending e-mail to friends or business associates, or whether you wish to fully access all the Internet has to offer, including the creation of an electronic storefront.

Keeping in mind that the Internet is a collection of computer networks, all of which, connected together, form one very large global computer network, to gain access to the Internet you must *plug* your computer into it somewhere along the lines that form the network. This task is somewhat akin to adding an extension phone to your existing home phone wiring system: You would "break" into the existing wiring, add an outlet, and then plug your extension phone into the new outlet.

Direct Access

This is recommended only for folks with lots of money, time, and knowledge.

With the appropriate high-end computer system, a special high-speed telephone line from the phone company, various software programs, a few weeks or months of spare time, the correctly trained computer whiz kid (who truly understands how to use these resources to gain access), and some serious cash, you can create a direct access link to the Internet. This link would be "on" and functional for as long as your computer is turned on.

The advantages of having a direct link are:

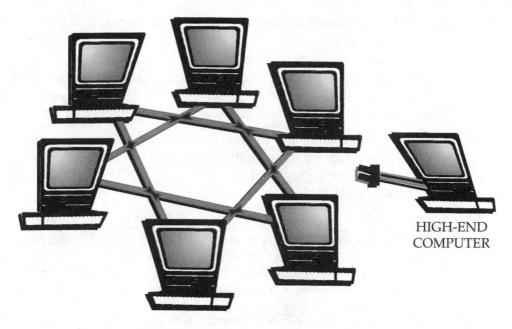

HIGH-END
COMPUTER

❏ *Speed:* You are able to travel the Net and upload and download files as fast as your modem and phone line can operate. With today's ultrafast modems and high-speed phone lines, you can operate literally at the speed of light.

❏ *Control:* Since you own the equipment and the whiz kid works for you, whenever you experience a technical problem, the solution is usually within your control and ability to correct in a timely manner.

❏ *Security:* Because you own and control the computer providing you with access to the Internet, it is not likely that you will unexpectedly lose your access due to the actions of others.

❏ *Storefront design:* Since you own the equipment and materials necessary to create an electronic storefront, and since the whiz kid works for you, how your electronic storefront can look and operate is your call, not how some other software programmer thinks it should look and function.

❏ *Additional revenue creation:* For individuals who opt for the indirect access option and who reside in your general area, you can provide an "access service," whereby, for a fee, they can gain access to the Net, while generating revenue for your company.

The major disadvantages of having a direct link are:

❏ *Cost:* By the time you purchase all the resources, you can easily spend well over $100,000. Obviously, this is a major investment for the small business owner or entrepreneur.

❏ *Time-consuming:* If you or your personnel are fairly new to computers, it could take you weeks or months to install and configure the equipment to gain access to the Internet.

❏ *Technologically difficult:* Considering the various advanced skills and knowledge base needed to set up a direct Internet access operation, it could be a major undertaking if you are not experienced in such matters.

If you would like to create a direct access link, here is a *basic* list of materials and resources that you would most likely need, as prepared by Mark Toleman, President of InterConnect West, an electronic storefront service developer:

Computer programmer/analyst	$50,000–$60,000 per year
T1 phone line	$25,000–$40,000 per year
Fast computer (i.e., Sun Sparcstation) with:	$20,000
At least 64 megabytes of memory	
4-gigabyte hard drive	
Terminal server or multiport serial device	
Router	
Channel services unit/data services unit	
UNIX software	
Other software	
Phone and fax machines	$2500
Phone lines (standard)	$2000–$4000 per year
General office equipment (desks, etc.)	$2000–$5000
Utilities (electric, etc.)	$4000–$6000 per year
Miscellaneous	$2500

At minimum, you're looking at investing over $100,000 to set up your own direct access. For the small business owner or entrepreneur, creating a direct access link to the Internet can be expensive and require a great deal of knowledge about hardware, software, and telephone systems. *While there are millions of large companies and organizations, and even some individuals who possess the needed resources and knowledge to produce such a direct link, such an access option is not recommended for the average small business owner and/or entrepreneur.*

If after reviewing both options you decide the direct access method is best for you, and if you are inexperienced in setting up an Internet location or storefront, take every precaution to enhance your chances of success. Seek out and find a consultant who can advise you beforehand as to what is necessary, who can act as your guide as the location is being developed, and who can then assist you when necessary in its daily use and operation.

Indirect Access

This is the recommended route for most small business owners and entrepreneurs.

Your cost is limited to that of a personal computer, a modem, and phone line, an inexpensive software program, and the paid services of an Internet access provider and an electronic storefront developer. In a relatively short time, you can set up your computer, install the necessary software, and have the developer create your storefront. You can then gain access to the Internet indirectly by connecting your computer to one that is already linked to the Internet.

Once you've connected your computer (often referred to as the *remote computer*) to a computer already part of the Internet (often referred to as the *host computer*), you can use the Internet in the same manner as if you had developed a direct access link. Actually, your computer is connected to the host computer via a standard phone line; with the appropriate software program installed on both computers and on both the host and remote modems controlling the linkage, you are actually connected into the Internet.

The major advantages of having an indirect access, as compared to direct access, are:

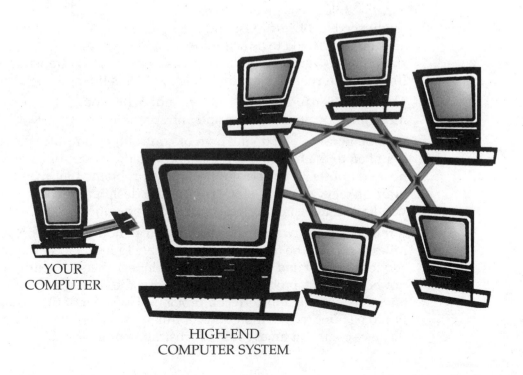

YOUR
COMPUTER

HIGH-END
COMPUTER SYSTEM

❏ *Less expensive:* The entire cost of a personal computer system with an appropriate modem, software, a phone line service, and the fees to pay the storefront developer can range from $2,000 to $10,000 (depending on which options you prefer)—certainly well within the resources of most small business owners and entrepreneurs.

Note: Additional expenses may be required to develop a storefront location, and to maintain the use on a month-by-month basis of an Internet access service and storefront developer. But these fees usually do not substantially raise the investment cost necessary to develop an indirect access linkage.

❏ *Faster setup time:* Setting up the entire computer system, including configuring the access software program, can be accomplished in only a few hours. Having the storefront developed can usually be done in a matter of days or a few weeks, depending on the work schedule of the developer and on the actual design of the storefront.

❏ *Easier:* Even for someone inexperienced in the use of computers, setting up an indirect Internet access location is possible without a great deal of outside technical assistance.

The major disadvantages of having an indirect access are:

❏ *Speed:* While most links between the remote and host computers are established at 14.4 or 28.8 baud rates (see App. A, "Internet Glossary"), and are considered to be fast transmission rates, these rates are still substantially slower than the rates at which data can be transmitted to and from the Internet using a direct T1 line access linkage.

Note: A 28.8 baud rate is recommended for conducting business for most small business owners and entrepreneurs.

❏ *Control:* Because you do not own or control the computer that is actually linked to the Internet, you must rely on the owner or caretaker of the host computer to correct any technical problems that may occur with your linkage, as well as to carry out the design and content objectives you have established for your storefront operation.

If the distance between the host and your remote computer is only a few miles (as would be the case if you are able to find a local Internet access service provider and/or storefront developer), then the control issue may not be a serious problem. You could visit the host site if your personal attention is needed to correct a problem. However, if the distance turns out to be hundreds to thousands of miles, as is often the case, such long-distance control at times could be frustrating or impossible to implement.

❑ *Security:* Because you do not own and control the computer providing you with the access to the Internet, you could unexpectedly lose that access due to the actions of others. For example, if the owner of the host computer needs to shut down the system for maintenance or repair, or, worse, elects to go out of business without giving you notice, your access to the Internet could be interrupted or permanently terminated without your knowledge or control. Any loss of Internet access would mean a loss of business revenue!

Two kinds of indirect access service are available. You can gain access via any number of private Internet access service providers. These are private companies, large and small, that have the equipment and resources necessary to enable you to gain access to the Internet. A list of these providers can be found in the Chap. 9, "Internet Access Service Providers and Storefront Developers."

A second indirect access option is provided by most of the commercial computer network services, such as America Online, CompuServe, Delphi, PRODIGY, and others. At the time of this publication, none of the commercial services had installed *complete* access to the Internet. Complete access includes all the functions listed in the following section, "How Does One Travel on the Internet?" However, America Online, CompuServe, and PRODIGY all offer a variety of Internet options including access to Web sites.

Like all business ventures, setting up an electronic storefront comes with its share of risks. However, taking into consideration all factors, especially costs and time, we believe the use of the indirect *access option is preferred over that of a direct access method for the small business owner or entrepreneur. Therefore, the remainder of this book will deal exclusively with creating an electronic storefront through the use of an indirect access linkage (with the assistance of an electronic storefront developer).*

How Does One Travel on the Internet?

To travel the Internet, you can use any of the following communication options:

❑ E-mail
❑ File Transfer Protocol (FTP)
❑ Gopher

❏ Internet Relay Chat (IRC)
❏ Mailing Lists and Usenet News
❏ Telnet
❏ World Wide Web

Using your copy of NetCruiser, you can actually use the preceding options to visit any location you wish on the Internet, as well as to gain access to the wealth of information that exists online, and to visit electronic storefronts online. A basic description of each option follows.

If you wish to obtain a more detailed explanation of how to use each of these options, we suggest you purchase a copy of a book entitled *Access the Internet* by David Peal (Sybex Publishing—see App. C, "Internet Resource Directory" for more information). Peal's book describes in plain English how to use the NetCruiser software program to access and use the Internet functions. It is highly recommended!

To begin to understand these options, first consider an analogy using our current transportation system in this country. If you wanted to travel from New York City to Miami, you have several options. You could, for example, take a car, bus, train, plane, boat, motorcycle, or bicycle, or you could walk. Each of the options is different, having certain advantages and disadvantages over the other options. Each can be used to get from one location to another, but some will take longer and require more effort than others. Such is the case with the Internet options—but some options are better than others.

E-mail

From the very beginning of the ARPAnet and Internet networks, people have been using the e-mail (short for electronic mail) function to send messages back and forth to each other. E-mail has quickly become one of the most preferred methods of communication among individuals, whether they are in close proximity (such as in the same building), across town, or on opposite sides of the earth. See Fig. 1-3.

Messages sent using e-mail travel through the Internet as fast as a regular telephone call and, in certain cases, faster. Therefore, it's possible to send a message from Dallas, Texas, to Rome, Italy and back in only a matter of seconds. While the United States Postal Service can take days to deliver a letter across the country, and even the fastest Overnight Express Service takes hours to get a message (document) from one location to another, e-mail can get it there in only seconds.

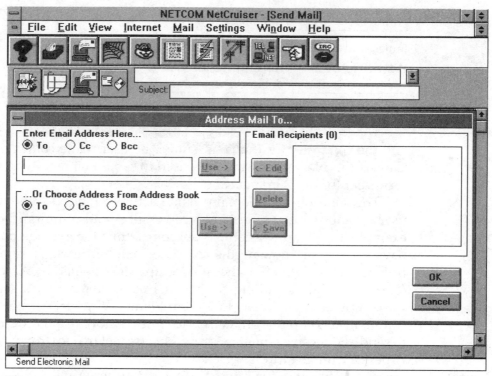

Figure 1-3. The NetCruiser e-mail function.

Another factor underlying the popularity of e-mail is its cost. You can e-mail a 50-page document from New York City to San Francisco for only a few pennies (i.e., the actual cost of the phone call). If you mailed it first class, it could cost several dollars. Such speed, ease of use, and cost savings offered only by e-mail are the main reasons for its growing popularity.

Central to the use of the e-mail function is the concept of an Internet address. Each computer connected to the Internet is assigned a unique name, and each person using each computer is also assigned a unique name. Therefore, it is possible to label an e-mail message with a specific Internet address to ensure that it will arrive at the correct destination (computer). All communication on the Internet is undertaken between at least two e-mail addresses: yours and the location where you wish to travel or the person to whom you wish to communicate.

Individuals can often have several Internet addresses if they are using several Internet access service providers with which to access the Internet. For example, you can reach the authors by using any of the following addresses:

Author	E-mail address
James Gonyea	careerdoc@aol.com
Wayne Gonyea	careerpro1@aol.com
	online@ns.cencom.net

The Internet address is divided into at least two parts, the user name and the computer (or domain) name. The user name comes first, such as CareerPro1. Next the @ symbol is used to separate the user name from the computer (or domain) name.

The computer (or domain) name actually identifies the name of the user's computer that sends and receives all e-mail communications. In our example, the computer name is aol.com. While the average person would have no way of knowing the computer name from such vague information, we can tell you that the AOL computer is owned by America Online (one of America's leading commercial computer network services), and the computer is physically located in Vienna, Virginia. As members of this commercial computer online service, the authors use their e-mail system to send and receive e-mail messages. Please feel free to drop us a line at our America Online address!

The .com extension refers to the fact that the America Online computer is a *commercial* business service. Other domain extensions include the following:

Extension	Meaning: The computer is …
.edu	part of an educational institution.
.gov	part of a governmental institution.
.mil	part of a military institution.
.org	part of some private organization.
.net	part of an organization that administers a computer network.
.ca	located in Canada.
.uk	located in the United Kingdom.

What this all means is that, if you were to send Wayne Gonyea a message using his America Online e-mail address, your message would first travel from your computer, through several routers, until it ultimately reaches the America Online computer located in Vienna, Virginia. From there it would be saved internally on the America Online computer, and sent to the CareerPro1 account. When Wayne next logged onto the America

Online service, your e-mail message would be waiting for him in his e-mail in-basket. Naturally, to accomplish this feat, you would have to have a computer that has e-mail access to the Internet.

When you create your electronic storefront (covered later in this book), you'll use the e-mail function often to communicate with all kinds of people on the Internet and other computer network services, such as customers, vendors, and the general public who may wish to contact you for information about your products and services. If you're like most people, you'll quickly agree that the use of e-mail is superior to the conventional United States Postal Service, and even the fax machine in certain situations.

Your copy of NetCruiser included with this book contains an excellent e-mail system for sending messages electronically.

File Transfer Protocol (FTP)

Almost as common as the e-mail function on the Internet is the practice of electronically sending files back and forth from person to person. The process of sending files is known as File Transfer Protocol (FTP). See Fig. 1-4.

Using FTP you can:

❑ Send a file (commonly referred to as *uploading* a file) from your computer to another person's computer on the Internet.

❑ Retrieve a file (commonly referred to as *downloading* a file) from another person's computer to your own and save it for future reference.

With the FTP function, you can upload or download a variety of files, such as files that contain:

❑ Graphics.

❑ Photos.

❑ Software programs (executable programs).

❑ Sound clips.

❑ Text information.

❑ Video.

When you consider the power and speed of FTP, why would you even consider sending such items the old way (United States Postal Service), when you can upload or download these items in only a matter of seconds or minutes using the Internet and FTP? Naturally, the sender and receiver both have to have an Internet address for the FTP process to function.

Considering the millions of computers already connected to the Internet, you can find thousands and thousands of files available for

Figure 1-4. The NetCruiser FTP function.

downloading, most of which are free of charge. As a matter of fact, many of the files that are "out there" on the Internet may contain information and resources that you can use to foster the development of your business.

As a businessperson working from an electronic storefront, you can use FTP to upload files to customers, employees, consultants, etc. containing such items as:

❑ Product catalogs.

❑ Annual sales report.

❑ Company telephone log.

❑ A copy of the slick new television commercial you just had created.

❑ A picture of the company building and personnel.

❑ A copy of your company logo.

❑ Press releases.

❑ New product update announcements.

❑ A training video.

❑ A copy of your latest software program.

You can also download files from the same individuals to your computer.

If you are like most Internet users, you will find that you download far more files than you upload. This is true simply because of the vast numbers of files available for downloading. When you want to download files from a remote computer, you'll need to know the following information:

❑ The Internet address of the remote computer

❑ The name of the file you wish to download

❑ The mode you should set your FTP program in order for the file to transfer properly (such as binary or text)

Your copy of NetCruiser provides you with a special program, called Archie, that becomes available when you call up the FTP function. Archie is an Internet search program, and can be used to search the Internet landscape to first find files that match your interests and needs, and then to obtain the necessary information with which to set your FTP program for proper file transfer (downloading).

Once you have identified files at remote sites that you want to download, you'll use the FTP function to access those sites. When you actually reach the site, the remote computer will normally ask you to log in (a process of identifying yourself by typing in your name and perhaps a password that you create). This is often necessary as many computer site owners, for security purposes, want to know who's accessing their information.

Rather than having to enter your name in each and every time you visit a remote site, you can instruct FTP to transfer the files anonymously. This means that FTP will identify you to the remote site only by your Internet address (which does not reveal your identity). However, if the remote site owner ever needs to get in touch, he at least has an Internet address. Once connected to the remote site, you can then begin the process of transferring files to the remote site (uploading) or from the remote site (downloading).

While you are in fact controlling the remote computer to some degree, it is only for the purpose of transferring files. You will not have access to the other data and programs stored on the remote computer. To be able to take more control over the remote computer, and actually control the remote computer as if you were sitting in front of it using it's keyboard, see the section devoted to Telnet.

As a businessperson using the Internet, you'll find the FTP function to be a most useful and valuable resource, and your copy of NetCruiser contains all the FTP power you'll need to upload and download files.

Gopher

Somewhat akin to the Archie search program, which you use when finding files with the FTP function, Gopher is yet another search program designed to help you find the information you're looking for on the Internet. See Fig. 1-5.

When you use the Gopher program, you're actually sending a message out on the Internet to several thousand special machines called Gopher servers, that contain information about resources available on the Internet. When your message is received by a Gopher server, a special software program, called Veronica, can be used to search the server's database to determine if it has any information on the topic in which you're interested. If it does, then that information is returned to you to help identify the location on the Internet where the information you want can actually be found.

All found information is then displayed on your computer screen in the form of topic menus. You can then easily scroll through the menu system, select the topic or topics that you would like to view or download, and then select a special button to actually visit the site or download the file.

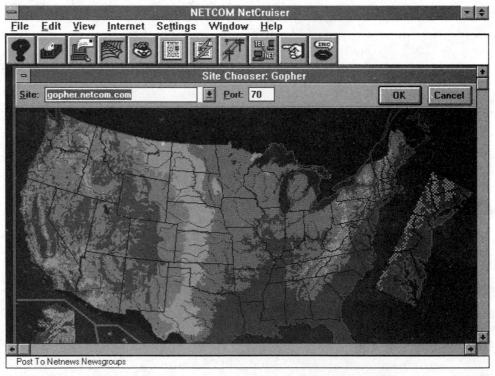

Figure 1-5. The NetCruiser Gopher function.

As stated in the FTP section, you are likely to download many files considering the vast number of files available on the Internet, most of which are free of charge. As a businessperson with little time on your hands for searching for information, you'll turn to Gopher often when you need information to help run your business enterprise.

Your copy of NetCruiser has an excellent Gopher search function.

Internet Relay Chat (IRC)

Most of the interaction occurring on the Internet is a matter of viewing on screen some form of "canned" or "stored" information that was previously created by another individual and left there for your viewing. The time will come, however, when you will actually want to talk—in real time (i.e., as it is happening)—with someone on the Internet. This is possible with a function called Internet Relay Chat (IRC). See Fig. 1-6.

Whether you're interested in social conversation, or wish to discuss a business matter, IRC provides you with the mechanism to have a group or "private" conversation in real time.

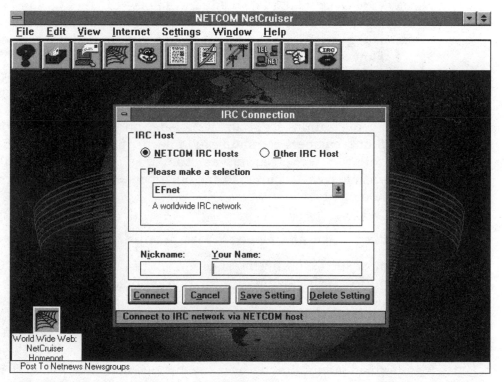

Figure 1-6.   The NetCruiser IRC function.

The computer used to gain access to the Internet is referred to as a *server*. If you have a direct connection to the Internet, then the computer you're using or connected to is the server. If you have an indirect access to the Internet, then the computer that your computer "calls up" to gain access to the Internet is the server, not your own computer.

Each server has special software to support IRC conversations. If the access software you are using to reach the Internet also supports IRC, then you can engage in conversations online. NetCruiser provides you with an excellent IRC program for chatting online.

When you call up the IRC function, you actually will have access to the several *channels* of conversation. NetCruiser gives you up to five channels of conversation. Think of a channel as a station on the radio dial. If you change the channel you can then chat with a different group of individuals. You can either join in the conversation that's already going on, just sit back and "listen" without contributing, or send private messages to specific individuals who are part of the selected channel.

You can create a "private" or "secret" channel if you wish to have a one-on-one conversation with an individual or group of individuals. However, while your conversation is private as far as other Internet travelers are concerned, system administrators who monitor and manage the server or servers that are used to transmit your conversation could, if desired, gain access to your conversation without your knowledge.

However, system administrators do not hang around all day and evening peeking in on people's conversation; they too have their work to do. There's so much conversation going on that it would consume their entire workday and personal time to listen in. For all practical purposes, your conversations are secure to a degree and should be fine for most personal and business communication needs. However, just remember that they are not 100 percent private, so don't mention anything that you do not wish to have disclosed to any other person other than yourself and the intended party.

Mailing Lists and Usenet Newsgroups

As most successful businesspeople will tell you, one key to success is to keep up with current information published about one's industry. Understanding the trends, problems, resources, leading experts, and other such information about one's industry is paramount if you expect to succeed within your chosen field. However, this concept is far easier said than done. Today, it can become a full-time job just to keep up with the new information published each day by the many people (often millions) involved in an industry. See Fig. 1-7.

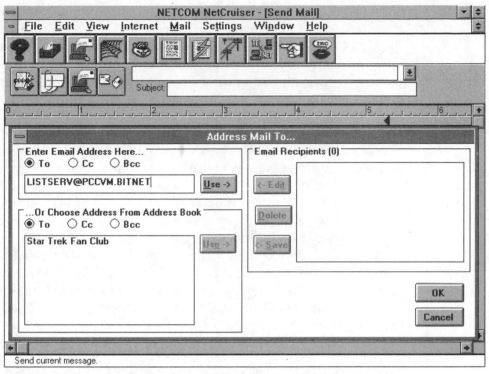

Figure 1-7. The NetCruiser Mailing Lists function.

In the good old days, one way of managing information often employed by business executives was to hire a news clipping service. Such a service would monitor various printed publications, such as magazines and newspapers. The clipping service would then forward information they found about any subject of interest to the business executive. Today, there's even a better option: Internet Mailing Lists.

Mailing Lists provide any number of Internet members with a means of sharing information about a subject. At last count, over 4000 different Mailing Lists were available on the Net.

Here's how it works. All individuals who wish to contribute their thoughts on a subject are invited to e-mail their thoughts to a list server (usually spelled as List Serv and usually a person or computer that manages the updating and mailing of the list). All e-mail that is received by the List Serv is added to a master document, and a copy of the document is then e-mailed back to each person who has registered with the list. Often the updating and mailing of the master document is done automatically by the List Serv's computer. Everyone on the list receives continual updates and has a copy of all comments made on the subject. Individuals who do not wish to contribute comments can still add their names to the list and receive copies of the master document.

By signing up with several Mailing Lists, you can keep track of what's going on in your various fields of interest. Many lists exist covering topics of interest and value to business owners. Also, you are invited to create a mailing list of your own as a means of sharing information about your industry and area of expertise.

Caution: Mailing Lists should not be created for the sole purpose of advertising your business service; such a practice would result in retaliation by many members of the Internet community. However, your business service can indirectly benefit as more and more people who receive your Mailing List will eventually become aware of your storefront.

Your copy of NetCruiser has a built-in feature for identifying and subscribing to any number of Mailing Lists.

Very similar to Mailing Lists are Usenet Newsgroups. Usenet Newsgroups are collections of articles available for downloading to your computer on just about every imaginable subject known to humankind. At last count, the number of Usenet Newsgroup articles exceeded 8000 topics! See Fig. 1-8.

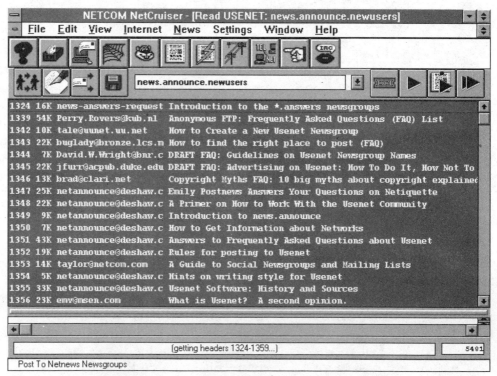

Figure 1-8.   The NetCruiser Usenet News function.

As with Mailing Lists, you may submit your thoughts to a Usenet Newsgroup by e-mailing your comments to the person who manages the Newsgroup in which you wish to join. Such a process is often referred to as *posting to a Newsgroup.*

Your submission, known as an article, is added to all the other submissions. All submissions are then made available to all Internet servers (the host computer through which you gain access to the Internet). Which Newsgroups you actually have access to is determined by the person who owns or manages the server to which you are connected. Most servers carry at least several thousand Newsgroups. When you launch NetCruiser, you will actually be connected to a server known as NetCom, and from that server you can access thousands of Newsgroups.

Also as with Mailing Lists, you may request articles without first submitting an article yourself. Unlike Mailing Lists, you do not send an e-mail message to a List Serv asking to receive regular updates to the Mailing List. Rather, you simply inquire of your host computer as to which Newsgroups are available to you, and then you may access and download as many or as few articles as you wish.

To review the many articles contained within a Newsgroup, and to actually read the articles themselves, you need a special software program called a Newsreader. Your copy of NetCruiser has an excellent Newsreader built into the program.

Using Newsgroups, you can tap into the vast information libraries and data files available on the Internet, a resource you'll likely use often when you need information to help run your business enterprise.

Telnet

Telnet (often mentioned as a means of conducting long-distance computing) is a marvelous function, available on the Internet, that allows you to actually log onto computers anywhere in the world, and then access or control the data and programs (often with some restrictions) that are stored on the remote computer from the convenience of your own computer keyboard. See Fig. 1-9.

Why would you want to do this you ask? No matter how large or well stocked with information your own personal computer is, the time will come when you want—or need—access to more information.

For example, suppose you've heard rumors through your business grapevine that the government of Argentina might be interested in buying agricultural equipment, which you sell. You need information quickly on the grain production capability of Argentina to follow up on this lead.

To obtain this information, you could visit all your area public and college libraries, or maybe travel to a major city, such as Washington, D.C. But

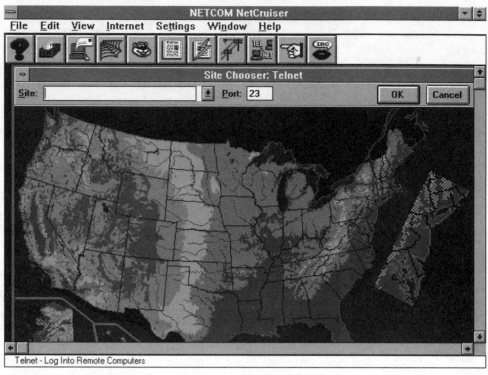

Figure 1-9.   The NetCruiser Telnet function.

why? With Telnet you can access some of the best card catalogs at many of the largest libraries in the country from your own personal computer using the Internet. Why go to the data, you can make the data come to you!

By Telneting to another computer located on the Internet, and by logging in (identifying yourself and perhaps entering a password), you can then take over control of the remote computer and access the data you wish. Telnet is similar in concept to FTP in that you can gain access to data stored on a remote computer. However, with Telnet, you can have more control of the remote computer other than just file transfer, as is the case with FTP.

If you know the name of the Telnet location where you wish to travel, you simply start the Telnet program, enter the correct address, and instantly jump through cyberspace down the Internet until you reach the desired Telnet location. However, if you're looking for certain information and think it could possibly be found on a remote Telnet computer, but you're not sure which one, you would use any of several special search programs (Hytelnet or LIBS) to first determine if such information exists, and at what location.

Your copy of NetCruiser provides you with full access to the vast resources available on the Internet via the Telnet option.

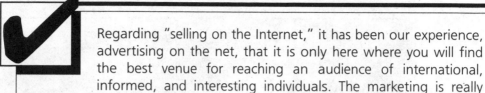

Regarding "selling on the Internet," it has been our experience, advertising on the net, that it is only here where you will find the best venue for reaching an audience of international, informed, and interesting individuals. The marketing is really about people in a global sense. It is personal and, ultimately through the process of e-mail, an experience in communication and understanding. We have found the process totally rewarding. A growing market with financial benefit in universal commerce.

Visi-Tech, Inc. has found a niche. It's about persistence and tenacity. You find a site or a virtual mall, and then settle in. Patience is important. If you stay aware of the ever-changing what's-new sites and manage to become a part of the new postings, then you will be discovered. The real challenge on the commercial net is simply to be found … it's a huge web.

Jeanne Housman
Director
Visi-Tech, Inc.
visitech@tiac.net
http://www.tiac.net/users/visitech/home.html

World Wide Web: The Best the Net Has to Offer!

If any function on the Internet is exciting, intoxicating, and habit-forming, it's the World Wide Web (WWW), usually referred to as the *Web*. Play around with this way of traveling the Net for just a few minutes and you're hooked! For those individuals interested in traveling the Net just to discover new and fun locations, or the dead serious businessperson interested in setting up shop online, the Web is the place to be. And it's getting bigger, better, and more popular every day! See Fig. 1-10.

So what is the Web?

On the computers scattered throughout the Internet you can find "information" of all kinds that the computers' owners, or the individuals they represent, wish to share with you. With millions of computers connected to the Net, there's no shortage of information available for your use—from personal to business-related information. If it's not out there today, it will probably be tomorrow! In short, thousands of people want you to visit their Internet location (computer) to see what they've posted online.

See Chap. 8, "Actual Storefronts in Use Today," to view many of the locations on the Internet where your presence is invited.

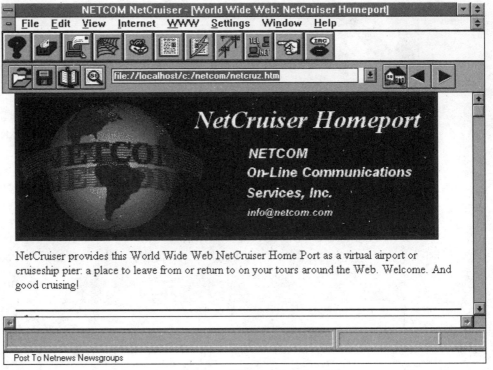

Figure 1-10.   The NetCruiser World Wide Web function.

Information available on the Internet can be displayed on your computer monitor in either of two formats:

❑ *Textual:* Only words appear on screen (such as what can be accessed using the Telnet option).

❑ *Graphical:* Graphics, pictures, text, and other elements appear on screen, which better appeal to your senses than text alone.

The Web is the function of the Internet that can display graphical information, and because of this has become more popular than non-Web functions with millions of users.

If you're like most people, you'll agree that textual displays are much less attractive—even boring—when compared to today's highly graphical screen displays. You're much more likely to watch a screen display that involves more of your senses, than just reading printed words on screen. And that's exactly why a graphical format is used by so many people posting information online—to attract you to visit their Internet location. The difference between text and graphic displays may seem trivial to some readers, but it is the main reason why so many entrepreneurs have chosen the Web function over the other means of traveling the Net as the prime location on the Net from which to conduct business.

With today's high-speed advanced computers, various kinds of "information" can be displayed on screen. For example, with the right equipment, all the following forms of information can be displayed *simultaneously* on your computer monitor:

❏ *Text:* Written words

❏ *Graphics:* Computer-drawn artwork

❏ *Photos:* Actual 35-mm quality photographs

❏ *Sounds:* Sound clips

❏ *Animation:* Images that appear to move

❏ *Videos:* Actual movies or clips from movies

If you've seen any of the recent CD-ROM computer programs published over the last few years, such as Microsoft's Encarta (an encyclopedia program), then you're familiar with software programs that display all such information simultaneously on screen, programs generally referred to as *multimedia software*.

Appealing to both our visual and auditory senses, and involving us in an interactive process (where you actually control the computer program making it do what you want it to do, rather than vice versa), these multimedia programs are far more enjoyable to use than the older "text only on screen" programs popular in the recent MS/DOS era.

This same kind of multimedia experience can now be achieved on the Internet when using the Web function. Actually, the Web is still in its early stage of development when it comes to the use of multimedia programming. To achieve true multimedia on the Web requires certain advanced equipment not normally used by the average person, but the process has clearly started and will continue to advance in the months and years to come. All things being equal, if you have a choice of visiting two sites to access the same information, where one incorporates a multimedia format and the other does not, chances are good that you'll travel to the multimedia Web location.

But multimedia is not all that's great about the Web!

In addition to offering Internet visitors a multimedia experience, the developers of a Web location can also link various text and graphical objects (i.e., buttons, arrows, pictures, drawings) on their main computer screen (using a function called *Hypertext Links*) to related text found elsewhere in the same document (see Fig. 1-11), in other documents on the same computer, or even in other documents found on other computers on the Internet, to enable the viewer to quickly jump to a related topic. (See Fig. 1-12.)

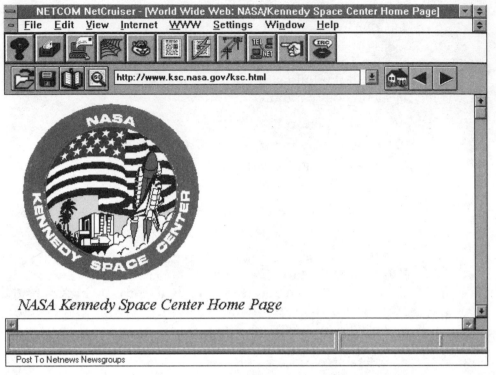

Figure 1-11.   Home page of a Web site that offers Hypertext Links (see Fig. 1-12) to additional pages.

Notice in Fig. 1-12 that several words are <u>underlined</u>. This means that they have been hypertexed, and if selected (clicked on with your mouse), will take you to some other location (as determined by the creator of this storefront) where you can find related information on the same subject.

Hypertext Links allow you to follow a predetermined line of thought when searching for information, rather than having to hunt for the information yourself in a straight and linear fashion from page to page.

Think of these Hypertext Links as bookmarks or footnotes found in traditional printed publications. A bookmark or footnote can be used to indicate that additional information about the marked word or phrase is available if desired elsewhere in the publication, usually at the bottom of the page, at the end of the chapter, or at the back of the book.

Unlike the printed word, electronic hypertexed documents can allow you to jump immediately to related information anywhere in the same or separate documents on the same computer, or to related information on a computer on the other side of the planet. If the Hypertext Links are designed properly, they can be an easy and convenient means of following

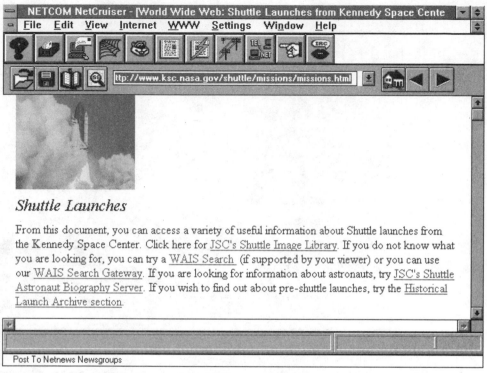

Figure 1-12. Web site page with Hypertext Links.

a single idea trail, enabling you to gather as much information as you wish quickly without having to read through volumes of unrelated information.

To view Web locations on the Net, special software is required, generically referred to as a *Web browser*. Several excellent browsers exist on the market today, including the browser contained within your copy of NetCruiser.

To travel to a specific Web location, you need to know its Web address. This is referred to as URL (uniform resource locator). For example, the URL of one of the author's electronic storefronts is:

    http://www.icw.com/america/made.html

Understanding the meaning of all the parts of a URL address is not important at this time. Just remember that, by typing in such a Web location into a Web browser, you will be able to jump from your computer to the computer housing the location where you wish to travel, in this case Made in America!, an electronic storefront where some of America's best hand crafters display and sell their goods. See Fig. 1-13.

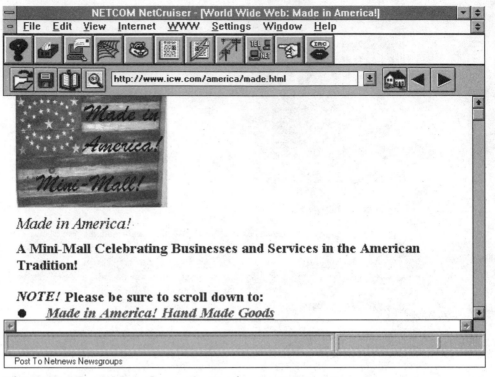

Figure 1-13. Wayne Gonyea's storefront.

Be careful: When typing in a URL address, make sure you use the proper case. The proper URL we just used is written as:

http://www.icw.com/america/made.html

However, if you were to change any of the text, such as the first letter in the word *america*, to upper case, such as:

http://www.icw.com/America/made.html

The connection could not be made. Unlike e-mail addresses where case is not important, it is critical with URLs.

When you reach a Web location, in this case a computer in Salt Lake City, Utah, the first thing you encounter is the location's *home page*. From the home page, you can then jump, using Hypertext Links, to other information on the same computer, or back to some other location on the Internet.

By jumping from one computer to another, you can literally travel the entire globe. This process of jumping from computer to computer, at almost the speed of light, is referred to as *cruising the Net* or *surfing the Net*, and is a very popular pastime once you learn the basics of its operation.

Summary

You now know how you can travel down the Internet. Don't be alarmed if you don't understand all the functions described in this chapter. There's a lot of new knowledge here, and it will take some time to become second nature. However, with practice you can become as comfortable traveling the Internet as you are driving down your neighborhood street.

Many newcomers to the Internet report that participation in a local seminar, workshop, or minicourse on the subject of how to use the Internet has helped them learn how to function better once online. Check the local schools and colleges in your area to see if any courses are being offered in your area. Also, check your video and computer stores for information about Internet courses, seminars, lectures, videos, and private consultants.

For now, however, just remember, you can disseminate or acquire information in various ways on the Internet from the convenience of your personal computer. Also, because of these Internet functions, you can conduct business online and market your products and services to the millions of people who also travel the same highway.

Now would be an excellent time to install and start becoming familiar with the NetCruiser software program. By getting online to the Internet and by personally checking out the landscape, you'll have a better understanding of how business is being conducted, and you'll be better prepared to learn how you too can start up your own storefront as outlined in the following chapters.

See you online!

2
Electronic Storefronts: The Internet Is Open for Business!

What Is an Electronic Storefront?

For those who prefer nontechnical definitions, consider an electronic storefront to be a location (i.e., an address) on the Internet from which you can electronically advertise and sell your commercial products and/or ser-

> ✓ The current revolution in information technology is very different from the traditional way we think of doing business. Electronic Commerce flattens the competitive landscape of business as we know it, enabling companies—large and small—to compete based on quality, value, product differentiation and customer education. Electronic commerce gives merchants access to the worldwide market for the price of a local magazine ad—a market which would be otherwise unattainable by small companies.
>
> **Shikhar Ghosh**
> Cofounder and CEO
> Open Market
> http://www.openmarket.com/

vices to other Internet users all around the world. For example, Fig. 2-1 shows a storefront that offers financial information for sale.

If you prefer a more technical definition, then think of an electronic storefront as the coexistence of two intangible entities—computer data and an electronic location for that data—for the purpose of conducting business electronically.

❑ In terms of *computer data,* everything that ultimately becomes your electronic storefront (whatever appears on screen, such as your company logo, information about your company, your product catalog, etc.) is created by and stored on a computer system, either your computer or a computer belonging to the company providing you with access to the Internet.

❑ In terms of *electronic location,* the computer containing your storefront data is connected to the Internet network, and therefore enables any individual on the Internet who wishes to visit your storefront location to access that data.

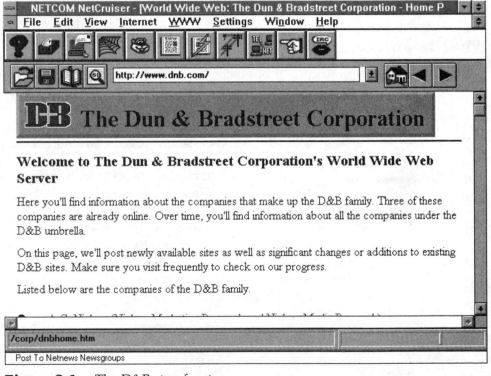

Figure 2-1. The D&B storefront.

In the sense that they can help you advertise your products and services to potential customers (in this case the part of the general buying public that has Internet access), electronic storefronts are similar to other traditional forms of advertising such as:

❏ Printed brochures and flyers.

❏ Printed catalogs.

❏ Printed magazine and newspaper display ads.

❏ Radio and television commercials.

❏ Posters and billboards.

However, unlike traditional methods of advertising, electronic storefronts do not stop delivering your message or disappear from view after the sales pitch has been delivered (as is the case, for example, with newspaper print advertising). In fact, storefronts remain alive indefinitely, continuing to deliver your sales pitch for as long as you wish to advertise or for as long as customers wish to view your message. Electronic storefronts also provide customers with a multimedia-based, interactive means of communicating with you, including the processing of sales orders.

Actually, if the definition of an electronic storefront includes disseminating your business message or ad, then conducting business on the Internet could also be accomplished using e-mail, Mailing Lists and Newsgroups, Internet Relay Chat (IRC), and Telnet, since all these functions can be used to disseminate information. However, these forms of communication offer less spectacular ways of delivering your message, and some actually produce negative responses from the Internet community if used for business purposes. For the same reason that Macy's dresses up its New York City storefront windows (to draw your attention and encourage you to enter and shop), the use of the Web and its multimedia capabilities is much more attractive for conducting business than any of these communications functions.

Electronic storefronts open an entirely new advertising medium for business leaders, one with advantages superior to traditional advertising options, and one that promises continual growth and use by the business community.

Before the Dawn of Electronic Storefronts

Ten years ago the Internet was a haven for highly skilled, technically trained computer programmers, analysts, technicians, and other scientists involved in research projects sponsored by the federal government, in particular the Department of Defense. At one time, little to no commercial business activity could be found on the Internet, since it was considered a communication network for military research, science, and educational purposes only.

But Oh, What a Difference a Decade Can Make!

While a sizable portion of the Internet community today is still composed of professional educators and scientists affiliated with colleges and universities, some of which are supported by federal defense grants and who continue to use the Internet for nonbusiness applications, the fastest growing segment of the population is composed of private individuals and commercial business users. Considering the millions of dollars the business community is investing in the Internet, there is no question that business leaders will play a major role in shaping its future from this day forward.

Like any new business frontier where profit can be made, business leaders—both large and small—and entrepreneurs of all kinds will flock to set up shop along the uncharted roads of the Internet in hopes of realizing the American dream. As with all business ventures, some businesses will succeed, while others will fail, but even the failures will help to establish a climate ripe for future business in this new "land" of opportunity. In the long run, doing business will become as commonplace a function on the Internet as it is at our local shopping malls.

Statistics, Please!

How many businesses have set up shop on the Internet? Unfortunately, there is no easy way to answer this question. Since no central registration procedure is required of new businesses that elect to set up shop, and since the Internet is so vast (with over 50 million computers already connected), it's next to impossible to determine how many businesses currently call the Internet their office location.

However, from a review of various articles on the subject, after hours of surfing the Internet to identify companies that have set up shop, and from conversations with various individuals and organizations who attempt to monitor such activity, it is clear that thousands of companies have already opened their electronic doors, with thousands of new businesses coming onboard each month. For those individuals familiar with the Internet community, it's no longer a question of whether the Internet will become a viable location for conducting your business, but more a matter of when you will open your storefront.

For some businesses that need an edge to survive in the marketplace, the use of the Internet could be a critical factor. As recently reported by Patricia Seybold, "If you're not an active Internet citizen by the mid 1990s, you're likely to be out of business by the year 2000."

One indicator of the growth of online business is the number of electronic *shopping malls* (i.e., cybermalls) that are popping up all over the Internet. A *cybermall* is a location on the Internet where information about various online businesses can be found, or where the actual storefronts of various businesses can be accessed. Similar to conventional shopping malls found in cities around the world, a cybermall provides you with an opportunity to visit a large number of stores without having to "drive" all over the Internet looking for products and services.

One of the largest and most successful malls is CommerceNet, a California-based service with a URL address of http://www.commerce.net/. It offers visitors access to many varied and different online storefronts. See Fig. 2-2.

Figure 2-2. CommerceNet storefront.

Embrace the New Technology

Whenever new technology comes along, some people flock to its use, while others shy away out of fear or ignorance. Can you imagine that many people actually feared and hated the telephone when it was first invented, and refused to incorporate its benefit into their personal and business lives. Today, the phone is an integral part of our personal and business lifestyles.

For those business individuals who have not yet mastered the basics of using a computer and accessing computer online network services, the likelihood of capitalizing on the opportunities that await on the Internet is slim.

Understanding how to use a computer and computer online services is not a technically difficult task, as some people would have you believe. Certainly, if children with a little formal training can operate a computer, then adults can as well.

If you lack an understanding and feel incompetent, consider using any of the following options to advance your knowledge:

❑ Read a book on computer use.

❑ View computer video tapes.

❑ Work one-to-one with a computer trainer.

❑ Attend a class or workshop on using computers.

❑ Ask a friend to teach you a few basic operations.

Whatever you do, don't put off upgrading your computer skills. The computer is the *power tool* of the twenty-first century. Fewer and fewer businesses and business executives, professionals, and office workers can expect to succeed without understanding computer applications.

Some people have convinced themselves that they can continue to succeed in their line of business without learning anything about using a computer. Such an attitude, we believe, is shortsighted, unrelated to the realities of the world and the future, and a sure formula for early retirement and possibly failure. The computer is here to stay and will become more and more a part of operating a successful business offline, as well as on the Internet.

Why Should You Open an Electronic Storefront?

As compared to opening a traditional store or office, opening an electronic storefront has many advantages. For example, by opening a storefront, it is possible for you to:

✓ *Increase your sales:* Since you're creating another sales outlet, you can expect the total number of sales of your products and/or services to increase.

✓ *Increase your market recognition and penetration:* With over 50 million people on the Internet today, more people will become familiar with your company, and the products and/or services you offer.

✓ *Reduce your operating costs:* Because it costs less to market and sell products and/or services from an electronic storefront than it does from a traditional storefront (office), your operating costs can be reduced.

✓ *Outsell the competition:* Because information about your products and/or services can be made available to potential customers worldwide in only a matter of seconds, you have the opportunity to put your goods in the hands of customers before your competitors.

✓ *Sell overseas:* Without having to open a traditional storefront in some country overseas, you can market and sell your products and services in all countries around the globe.

✓ *Operate from any location:* Because the display of your merchandise, and the actual sales transactions take place electronically online, you can operate from any location coast-to-coast, including, if you wish, your kitchen table!

✓ *Operate any time of the day or night:* With the Internet operating 24 hours per day, 7 days per week, 365 days per year without interruption (most of the time!), your storefront and therefore your business are open all the time, even while you're off playing, sleeping, or working at another job!

✓ *Run several unrelated business ventures:* While it might be difficult or undesirable in the traditional business world to operate several unrelated or conflicting business ventures from the same physical location, such as a financial investment service and a comic book trading store, it is possible on the Internet since you can open as many storefronts as you wish, with each store having its own separate and unique storefront.

✓ *Compete head-to-head with the corporate giants and still succeed:* Since all electronic storefronts are constructed of the same materials (computer graphics, text, etc.) and procedures, it is possible for the small "mom and pop" store owner or home-based entrepreneur to create a storefront that looks and operates like the ones created by corporate giants.

✓ *Inexpensively test out a business idea:* Without having to invest thousands of dollars on office space, furniture, advertising, personnel, etc., you can inexpensively test out the feasibility of your new business idea by opening a storefront.

✓ *Improve public relations and corporate communications:* Since your storefront is open to the general public around the clock, it can be used to post timely press releases, new product announcements, testimonials, and other such information that can improve your company's name recognition within your industry.

✓ *Provide a better and higher level of customer service:* While your normal office is closed part of the day and perhaps weekends, your electronic storefront can remain open to answer common questions asked by customers to better serve their needs.

✓ *Provide an automated central depository of information for staff:* When staff members are away from the corporate office, such as when attending a national sales meeting or when calling on distant customers, an electronic storefront can provide them with a convenient means of obtaining any variety of information, even if the corporate office is closed for the day or weekend.

In today's status-conscious society, having an Internet address and an electronic storefront is a clear sign to the world that you're on the leading edge of technology when it comes to doing business. In short, you have arrived!

What Types of Businesses Can Benefit from Opening an Electronic Storefront?

Just about any business! If you own and operate a business that produces a product or service that can be delivered to customers via any of the following methods, then you can also do business electronically:

❏ E-mail

❏ Fax

❏ Ground transportation, such as United Parcel Service (UPS)

❏ Overnight Express or next-day carrier

❏ Regular postal mail

Some products or services can not only be sold on the Internet, but also delivered electronically to customers. For example, if your company sells market analysis reports of companies doing business in foreign countries, such data could be delivered to customers electronically via e-mail or fax.

If your product or service cannot be delivered electronically, such as the case if you sell handmade ink pens, then your product can still be sold via the Internet, but you will have to ship your goods using conventional freight or mail services.

Here's a short list of some of the products and services that can be marketed via an electronic storefront:

- ❏ Accounting/bookkeeping service
- ❏ Antiques
- ❏ Artistic watercolor paintings
- ❏ Artwork
- ❏ Athletic equipment
- ❏ Bed and breakfast lodging resorts
- ❏ Boats and yachts
- ❏ Business billing service
- ❏ Business opportunities for sale
- ❏ Classic automobiles
- ❏ Computer equipment
- ❏ Desktop publishing services
- ❏ Electronic equipment
- ❏ Employment information
- ❏ Exotic animals
- ❏ Financial investment reports
- ❏ Hand-sewn or -crafted items
- ❏ Hand-crafted furniture
- ❏ Legal advice
- ❏ Medical reports
- ❏ Model train collections
- ❏ Musical instruments
- ❏ Real estate
- ❏ Sports card collections
- ❏ Sports equipment
- ❏ Sports memorabilia
- ❏ Stained glass creations
- ❏ Television programming transcripts
- ❏ Temporary employment referral service
- ❏ Travel information
- ❏ Unusual, one-of-a-kind items

The list can go on and on!

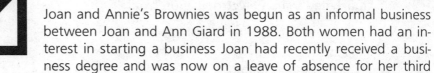

Joan and Annie's Brownies was begun as an informal business between Joan and Ann Giard in 1988. Both women had an interest in starting a business Joan had recently received a business degree and was now on a leave of absence for her third child. Ann, then a full-time student, was also on a leave of absence with a brand new baby. To both women, it seemed like an ideal time to experiment with a small business. At Ann's suggestion they chose to develop a brownie business. One of the key elements in the decision was that brownies had a remarkable shelf and storage life for a food product. This one decision would turn out to be a key element in the post Internet success story of the business.

After a great deal of effort they settled on a recipe for a very fudgy, chocolaty, brownie base and developed a series of delicious toppings. At a local food festival, they met a retired salesman, George Chamberlain. After a lifetime as a food service salesman, he knew he had recognized a product with special appeal

In April of 1990, the three formed a corporation, took out a business loan to purchase packaging, and formed a loose partnership between their corporation and a production facility called Rhino foods. The objective of the partnership was to assign production to a third party, Rhino, and allow the small company to dedicate its full-time efforts to marketing. The initial concept was that a gourmet, labor-intensive product could be introduced to the restaurant community as a generic brownie and to the consumer as a prewrap over the counter. Despite some initial promising sales, the product's inherently high-cost production overhead, could not compete with the lower-cost, high-volume, over-the-counter market. In addition, the restaurant service market, although successful for the restaurants, insulated the company from its clientele, since the brand name, Joan and Annie's, was not always mentioned on the menu. Finally, the market was essentially price-driven.

Problems abounded. In analyzing the company's current position there was one clear feature: The product was outstanding. The question was how to deliver a gourmet desert to the public directly without opening a restaurant or bakery? This seemed to be the only way to pay for the high production costs of a gourmet desert and to gain name recognition.

The first step was to turn the company's point-of-purchase box into a gift box for gourmet brownie lovers. This step then made possible the first of two key marketing decisions. They happened to note that one of the fastest growing businesses in the United States was another Vermont company, Vermont Teddy Bear. Taking a cue from that company, Joan and Annie came up with the idea of a Brownie Gram™. The Brownie-Gram would couple a gourmet desert product with a personal message and color computer graphics. In the era of information packaging and transfer, it was a new twist on top of a gourmet desert that could withstand the rigors of mail order shipment. The initial decision to choose a durable product had been a wise one.

But how to market this concept? By this time, Ann and her husband Chris were now the only partners in the company. Funds were limited. Chris had an avid interest in computers, first as a programmer and later as a physician. He had thought that Internet might be a cost-effective way of getting the word out for a business with limited capital. By serendipity he met the marketing director of a local concern with an Internet server dedicated solely to Vermont products. The company's name was Cybermalls of Colchester, Vermont. For a modest investment of $500, Joan and Annie's opened an Internet shop on the Cybermall. The shop consisted of five graphic pages that Internet users could browse through.

Within two months the company had begun to get inquiries from around the world. While the number of orders was not large, word was beginning to get out that a small company in Vermont had a Brownie-Gram.

The partners would soon see that the first success of their Internet decision was not the sale but rather the recognition in other parts of the country and world that the product was available. One of the Cybermall executives called to say that Joan and Annie's had even been mentioned in the *New York Times.*

Indeed, in an article in the *New York Times* Business Section, the two partners, Ann and Chris, found their small company mentioned alongside giant Fisher Scientific, as a new company on the Internet. Knowing that lightning may strike only once, they called the local TV stations and sent a press release. The press release made the point that Internet might be a great equalizer for a small company. Was it possible to become known without spending millions of dollars in the age of Internet? An additional call was made to the Living Section editors of the *New York Times,* inviting them to taste the product. The results of this small Internet connection were in retrospect soon to be beyond their expectations.

Both TV stations were quite taken with the concept. One TV station— Channel 5, WPTZ of Plattsburgh, New York—sold the story to CNN. The *New York Times* chose to receive the product. In about two weeks the *Times* published a complete article reviewing 11 mail order Brownie companies. Four of the companies had complimentary reviews. Joan and Annie's was one of the four. The *Times* termed the Joan and Annie's products as "fudgy," "chocolatey," "extremely good," terming Ann's toffee bar version "first rate." The result was an overwhelming surge in orders on the company's MCI 1-800 number (1-800-LUV-BROWnies). Nearly 500 orders arrived in one week.

In reviewing the journey from a small company sporting a first-class gourmet confection to a company that now had its own gourmet clientele, the key points were obvious. The first was packaging the product under the company's own name and logo. Only in this arrangement was it possible to charge enough for the product to justify the labor intensity involved in making it. The second was identifying the primary customer, the gourmet desert lover. But this customer was not only a lover of deserts. They had a secondary need to send a message that could be heard in a crowded electronic world. The third point was marrying a traditional gourmet food item to the message-intense environment of the electronic world with the Brownie Gram concept. And the final step, was using the Internet connection as the cost-affordable way of finding clients all around the country, when the business was tucked away in the hills of Vermont.

As Chris stated in a television Interview on the subject, "It used to be that you had a business on Main Street. With Internet your business opens on the world." For this small company, it's happened.

Christopher R. Chase, MD
Co-Owner, Joan and Annie's Brownies
1-800-LUV-BROWnies
http://www.cybermalls.com/cymont/joan/index.html

Can Nonprofit Companies and Other Noncommercial Organizations Open an Electronic Storefront?

Yes! Creating a platform from which products and services can be sold is only one reason for opening an electronic storefront. Nonprofit organizations, charitable groups, social clubs, political organizations and politicians, schools and colleges, fraternal organizations, and other similar not-for-profit organizations are using electronic storefronts to better realize their mission objectives. See Fig. 2-3.

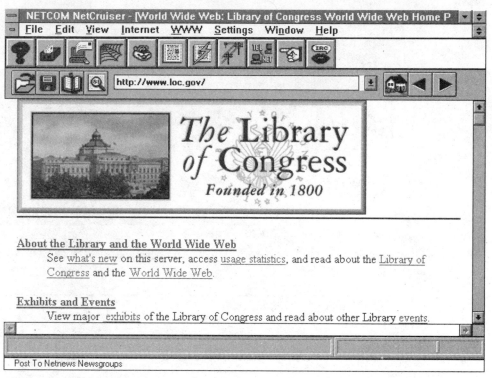

Figure 2-3. The Library of Congress storefront.

Actually, the use of an electronic storefront is an appropriate mechanism for any individual, group, or organization that wishes to disseminate information to the general online community. Appealing to many people who have an interest in publishing, creating an electronic storefront is an ideal, and dramatically less expensive, way of marketing a newspaper, magazine, or newsletter. See Fig. 2-4.

Unlimited Travel as Far as the Eye Can See

With no limit on the number of new people connecting to the Internet, with a technology that knows no boundaries in terms of growth, and with storefronts that can be anything you and a computer programmer can imagine, there seems to be no end to the number and kind of electronic storefronts that can be created.

Driven and created by the people who use it, the Internet will become what we all decide to make of it. So there's plenty of room for you to erect your electronic billboard and set up shop.

Figure 2-4. Major newspaper publishing on the Internet.

3

How to Open Your Own Electronic Storefront

When planning the development of your storefront, you will have to make many decisions, obtain resources, and manage the work flow either directly or by delegation to a co-worker. To help you keep track of your plans, a worksheet has been developed (see App. B, "Storefront Planning Worksheet"). It is suggested that you use this worksheet as a single, central location for recording your thoughts and plans. Whenever a thought occurs or when a question arises, you need only refer to this one location to keep track of all aspects of the project or to quickly find the answers needed.

Before You Begin

Prior to discussing the process of creating an electronic storefront, it would be wise to review a few preliminary thoughts to establish a mind set that is conducive to success.

Realistic expectations. Many entrepreneurs establish unrealistic expectations when it comes to the end result of setting up a new business, whether housed in a physical office location or an electronic storefront. Such expectations can lead to disappointment and, worse, financial loss.

Is it possible to do business on the Internet? Without question, yes! Can you generate profit? Yes, others have done it, we have done it, and we know it can be done! Will your venture be profitable? The answer to that question can only be perhaps!

Like any business venture, many factors influence the end result of your efforts, factors such as your drive, motivation, resourcefulness, the value of what you offer for sale, how you market and advertise your product or service, and the market demand for your product and/or services, just to name a few.

The small business and entrepreneurial landscape is littered with well intentioned, hard working individuals, with seemingly useful products and services, who, despite their best efforts, failed at their business. Succeeding at business is both a science and an art. No blueprint that we can offer will guarantee your success. Then again, nothing ventured, nothing gained!

Professor Sunil Gupta of the University of Michigan Business School, conducted a survey in 1994 of 3522 people who were using the World Wide Web to conduct business. What Gupta found is most interesting and a clue to how you can succeed with your own storefront. Gupta's findings indicated that Internet customers were using storefronts more to gather information about product and service buying options, rather than to actually order electronically. It seems customers would use storefronts to find information about products and/or services that they wished to purchase, and then went to traditional sales outlets to actually order the desired product or service.

Are such findings a positive predictor of the future of electronic storefronts or the first signs of another technology that failed to meet its expectations? Without question, Gupta's findings are good news!

Compared to the millions of business professionals and customers using the Internet today, 3522 respondents in 1994 may be considered only a drop in the bucket. The reality of what's happening with electronic shoppers today could be very different. However, Gupta's findings are important and should be considered when planning how to structure your electronic storefront. Gupta's findings imply that:

❑ You should position your storefront as an electronic catalog.

❑ You must make your products and services available through more traditional channels (such as from local store outlets, from a 1-800 service, etc.), as well as your storefront.

❑ You have to inform your Internet customers online about how they can order through traditional sales channels if that is their preference.

Our assumption.   As stated in Chap. 1, we assume you will be connecting to the Internet indirectly. Therefore, the advice given in this chapter will reflect the advantages and restrictions accompanying this option.

Kindred experience. To help you develop an appropriate mind set regarding what you are about to create, imagine that you are about to publish a multicolored printed catalog describing your company's product or service line, with information included regarding the cost of each item or service, background information about your company, and how to order by mail, fax, e-mail, or phone with the use of a credit card or check.

Such is the process you will complete to create your storefront. The only difference is that now your "catalog" will be interactive, changeable whenever desired, transmitted electronically around the world, and available to customers at any time of the day or night.

Unique concept. No two storefronts are alike and yours should be unique, reflecting the theme of your product or service line. Take the time necessary to create a storefront the reflects your business mission. Your storefront will make a very clear statement about who you are and what you have to offer. Make it an outstanding statement, one that will not soon be forgotten!

Professional appearance. Central to creating a storefront is the use of computer-generated graphics. Unless you are skilled at creating such graphics, hire a professional graphics illustrator to create the look of your storefront. Don't attempt to cut costs here, as you're likely to be disappointed with how your storefront looks on screen, and customers are less likely to be impressed and shop at your store.

Remember the 2×3 rule. As with many business ventures, the creation of your storefront may cost twice as much and take three times as long to develop than what the storefront developer you've selected has quoted.

A team approach. The demands of creating an electronic storefront are such that you may find it necessary to bring together several experts into a team. A typical team could consist of any or all of the following individuals:

❑ You, to act as the team manager
❑ A storefront development service, to create the storefront
❑ Graphic artist(s), to produce the screen graphics
❑ Information researchers, to find and collect the data you wish to display
❑ Word processing specialists, to prepare the hypertext documents (files)
❑ An Internet access service provider, to provide you with access to the Internet

It can be anticipated that the person that you will work most closely with to develop your storefront will be a storefront developer. See Chap. 9, "Internet Access Service Providers and Storefront Developers," for a list of such individuals and companies.

Long-distance management.   Considering the many people usually involved in creating a storefront, and the unusual fact that they are typically scattered across the country and do not all work in your local community, you'll often have to manage the process by phone. We strongly suggest you keep in touch with all parties daily to ensure a smooth development cycle.

Check references carefully.   You may have to work with service providers (i.e., graphic illustrators, storefront developers) who live and work in a distant community. So make sure you obtain references from those individuals and then call several to inquire as to the service provider's ability before you hire any individual. Failure to do so can result in a waste of your valuable time and money if the service provider fails to deliver the services contracted for. If the service provider cannot provide you with references, run—don't walk—to the next provider.

Get it in writing.   A lot can happen between the time you verbally (usually over the phone) agree with a member of your development team about how your storefront should look or operate and the time it actually goes live. Intentionally or unintentionally, changes will occur to your storefront, sometimes for good reasons, other times out of negligence. If you do not have your agreed-to terms outlined in writing and signed by all appropriate parties, you will have little ground to demand that your storefront be built as you requested. The last thing you want after weeks of work and thousands of dollars is a storefront that does not look and function as you anticipated.

First Learn How to Travel the Internet

Before you attempt to create your own storefront, you should understand how to function on the Internet. You should learn how to send and receive e-mail messages, how to transfer files using FTP, how to access Gopher and Telnet sites, how to chat online with IRC, how to use Mailing Lists and Usenet Newsgroups, and especially how to find and access World Wide Web locations, including existing electronic storefronts and malls.

If you have not already installed NetCruiser and begun to use these Internet functions, we strongly encourage you to do so now before attempting to complete this chapter.

If you are confused about how to install NetCruiser, or how to use the various Internet functions made available via the NetCruiser program, we strongly suggest you obtain the services of a computer tutor or instructor, and have that person show you how to use this program. Don't try to learn all about the Internet by yourself. It's too big and it will take you too long. And in business, time is money!

A few hours spent with a tutor will pay for itself time and time again as you will save countless hours of frustration, not to mention lost time and money trying to figure out on your own how to accomplish certain Internet tasks.

Storefront Design Elements

As a storefront owner, you will have the option to design your storefront to look and function any way you wish (within the limits of what is possible from a computer programming and systems point of view). The following list describes the elements that, together, can create an electronic storefront. You should review the list and decide which elements you wish to incorporate into your storefront. It is strongly recommended that you review this list with the storefront developer with whom you elect to work.

Most of these elements are mandatory and must be used. Optional elements have been labeled as such.

Use the Storefront Planning Worksheet to record your thoughts and questions about the elements you hope to include in your storefront.

❏ *Home page:* This is the first screen that visitors encounter when they travel to your Internet location. A storefront has only one home page. A home page may contain any or all of the remaining elements on this list (with the exception of the additional pages option). See Fig. 3-1.

Caution: Don't scrimp on the quality of graphic images on your home page. It's what your customers see first; it's the first impression they get of your storefront. You should do everything possible to make it a good first impression!

❏ *Additional pages:* These additional screens contain all the information that you wish to display within your storefront, and they are referenced by the Main menu system on your home page screen. You may create as many additional pages as you need. An additional page may contain any or all of the remaining elements on this list (with the exception of the home page option).

❏ *Banner with title:* In this element on your home page, you identify the name of your electronic storefront, usually with a graphic design as a background and the name of your storefront superimposed on the graphic. The use of any background banner or graphic is optional, but is usually included to present an attractive display.

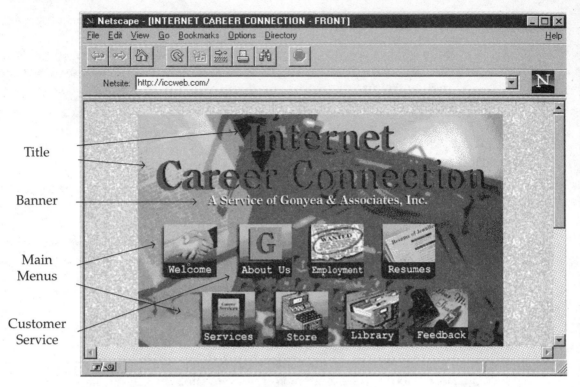

Title

Banner

Main
Menus

Customer
Service

Figure 3-1. Internet Career Conection home page.

Important: When using graphic images, do not attempt to install large images of the kind that would fill half or more of a page. Graphic images contain a great deal of data that computers have to read before the image can be displayed on screen, and therefore require a long period to download from the server (where your storefront will be located) to your computer or to your customer's computer. Long download times will frustrate many visitors, especially if they are paying an hourly access fee to use the Internet. The basic rule of thumb (until the majority of Internet users are using faster modems) is to keep graphics small. For reference sake, text can be downloaded at a much faster rate than graphics, video, photos, animation, and sound. The use of graphics should be discussed with your storefront developer, who should already be familiar with the correct size of images for fast downloading.

❏ *Subtitle* (optional): This element is often used to further define the purpose and content of your electronic storefront. Think of a subtitle here as having the same purpose as a subtitle for a book: to provide visitors with more information regarding the content or purpose of your storefront. The use of a subtitle is optional and, if included, is normally found only on the home page.

❏ *Main and submenus:* These elements (sometimes Hypertext Links) are used to inform visitors about the content of your storefront; they are a means of navigating through the various additional pages that comprise your storefront. A Main menu with accompanying submenus enables you to organize the content of your storefront into a convenient and meaningful hierarchical system. Visitors need only select the Main menu item that represents the information they wish to view or the location they wish to reach in order to properly use your storefront. As visitors select more and more submenus, they are allowed deeper access into your storefront and are presented with more and more specific information. The Main menu usually appears on the home page, and it (or a reduced version) may also appear on any number of additional pages to enable visitors to jump from any one location to another without having first to return to the home page. You may use any number of submenus you wish.

❏ *Customer service* (optional): This Hypertext Link element (see following description) is often referred to by several other titles, such as *Service, About [your storefront], Who We Are,* etc. Its purpose is to inform the visitor about the:

Owner of the storefront.

Name of the contact person.

Name of the company behind the storefront.

Company's mailing address.

Company's phone and fax numbers.

Company's e-mail address(es).

This element should be prominently displayed on your home page, often in a corner of the screen, and, when selected, it should display a new additional page containing the preceding information. Unfortunately, many storefront owners and developers fail to include this information, or bury it deep in a submenu. Such a practice usually results in frustration on the part of storefront visitors who wish to know how to contact you.

❏ *Help* (optional): When selected, this element takes the visitor to a different additional page, where information is displayed explaining how to complete the task that visitors encountered on the screen containing the Help element. Help buttons offer an excellent method of displaying optional how-to information when a complicated task or confusing information is presented on screen, and they can be included on the home page or any additional page.

For example, assume you include on one of your additional pages a fill-in-the-blank form that visitors could use to enter their names and mailing addresses to receive by mail a copy of your new Spring Product Catalog when it becomes available. To ensure that visitors understood the purpose of this form and the directions regarding how to complete it, you could add a Help element next to the form. Selecting Help causes a new page to appear containing the appropriate information and directions.

❏ *Hypertext Links:* See Fig. 3-2. This is the function that has made the World Wide Web so popular. Hypertext Links are words and graphics that are linked to related information located somewhere else within your storefront. These Hypertext Links are underlined (and in color) to indicate that such a link exists. Hypertext Links are contained within hypertext documents that are created with the use of a HTML (hypertext markup language) editor (explained later in this chapter), a software program similar in design to a word processing or text editor program.

When this element is selected, visitors are immediately taken to another page within your storefront where the related information may be

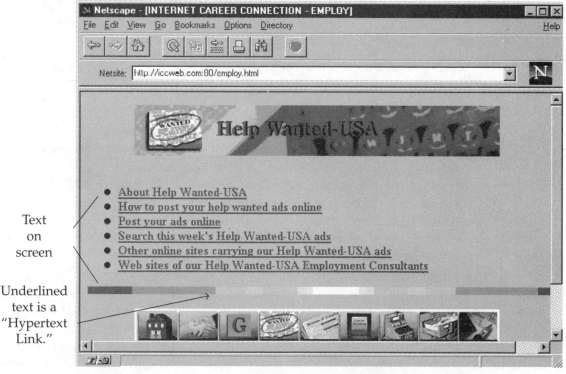

Text on screen

Underlined text is a "Hypertext Link."

Figure 3-2.   Internet Career Connection showing text on screen. Note: Text is also used as Hypertext Links.

viewed. If you prefer, you can link a word or phrase to any other store-front on the Internet. However, once you have taken the visitor to a new storefront, there's no way to guarantee that he will return to your location.

The use of Hypertext Links enables the storefront owner or developer to take a visitor down a particular *trail* or *thread* of information. Often, when a Hypertext Link is selected it turns a different color to indicate to the visitor that he has already traveled down that path.

❏ *Text on screen:* See Fig. 3-2. The most commonly used element, this element allows you to display printed information on screen (i.e., on a single page). A single page can hold an unlimited amount of text. If you include more information than what can be displayed on screen at any one time, the rest of your text may be viewed by selecting the down arrow on the scrolling mechanism.

All the text you see on screen for any storefront is also created with a hypertext markup language (HTML) program editor.

Caution: Creating long text pages is not wise, since many Internet users find it frustrating when forced to read through long scrolling screens to find the information they seek. It is much better to break the text into separate sections, each section contained on separate pages. By including a hypertext menu at the beginning of the first section, visitors can quickly jump to any section they prefer and, once there, scroll through the information quickly.

❏ *Graphics* (optional): These elements provide a colorful look or design to your home and additional pages to improve their overall appearance. See Fig. 3-3. As we all know, reading text on any printed page that is devoid of any artwork is often boring, as compared to reading text on a page that also has colorful artwork included.

Graphics are created with the use of any number of computer graphic illustration programs. These programs may be used by computer users who are not graphic artists, as well as by professional graphic artists and illustrators. While anyone with a little practice can create graphic "artwork," it is strongly recommended that you hire the services of a professional graphic artist to produce the kind of graphics that can enhance the look of your storefront.

The number and size of the graphics you include on any one page will determine how quickly that page can be downloaded from the server to your computer or to your customer's computer. The more graphics you use, and the larger they are, the slower the download will be. Your choice of graphics is something you should discuss carefully with your storefront developer.

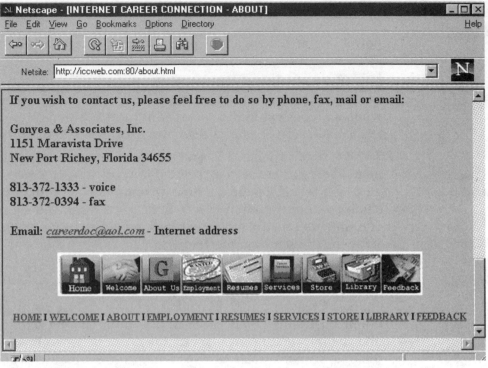

Figure 3-3.   Graphical Icon Bar used to navigate within the Internet Career Connection Web site.

❏ *Searchable database* (optional): See Fig. 3-4. A searchable database is a special computer software program that can store an unlimited amount of information about a particular subject, and that can then be queried by users in search of information.

For example, a searchable database located within a storefront called the Internet Career Connection contains information about employment opportunities (i.e., help wanted ads) made available to Internet travelers. The database contains approximately 15,000 individual ads each week. Each ad is considered to be a "record."

To identify ads that may be of interest, job seekers are instructed to enter a search word or phrase. If you were a job seeker interested in ads for "accountants," you would be instructed to enter the word "accountant." The program would then search each and every record. All records containing the word "accountant" would then be displayed on a list. You would then be able to view, save to a file, or print out a copy of any or all of the ads (records) found on the list. Because the program "searches" its records for you, searchable databases are an excellent way to provide detailed, comprehensive, yet specific information.

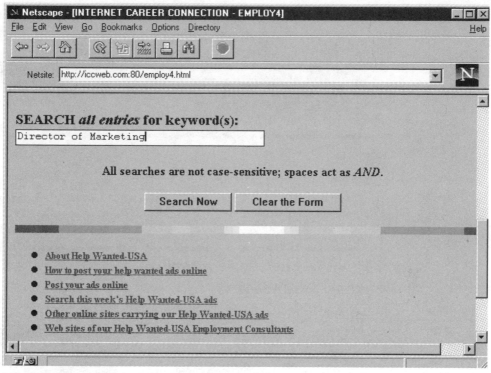

Figure 3-4.   Internet Career Connection's searchable database.

Naturally, all good things come at a price, and searchable databases are often much more expensive to create and install in a storefront than other elements. However, premade searchable databases are available for sale, and your storefront developer should be able to find existing programs that can be used (with or without editing). Otherwise, a skilled programmer can create one for you from scratch—for a fee.

❏ *Downloadable files* (optional): See Fig. 3-5. You may post in your storefront any number of files that visitors may download at their discretion to their computer. A file could contain any of the following:

Animation

Executable code (i.e., software programs)

Graphics

Photos

Sound clips

Text information (i.e., word processing documents)

Video clips

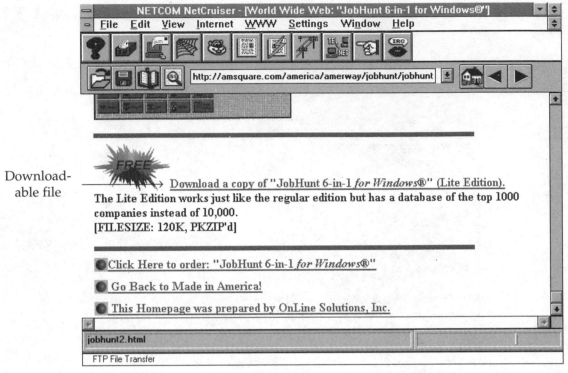

Downloadable file

Figure 3-5.   Made in America.

A downloaded file cannot be opened or its contents viewed or used on screen. To use a downloadable file, it must be first downloaded to the visitor's computer.

Depending on the contents of a file and the speed of your modem, the download time could be short or long. For example, a one-page text document could be downloaded in only seconds. However, a 90-minute video could take hours to download. Several compression programs exist that can compress a program to a smaller size to allow for faster download times. Two of the most popular compression programs are:

PKZIP (for use with PC computers).

Stuffit (for use with Macintosh computers).

As with graphics, your choice of which downloadable files to include should be discussed carefully with your storefront developer.

❑ *Fill-in-the-blank form* (optional): See Fig. 3-6. A fill-in-the-blank form is used to collect the information needed to process a customer's purchase. Normally, an order form collects the following information about the customer:

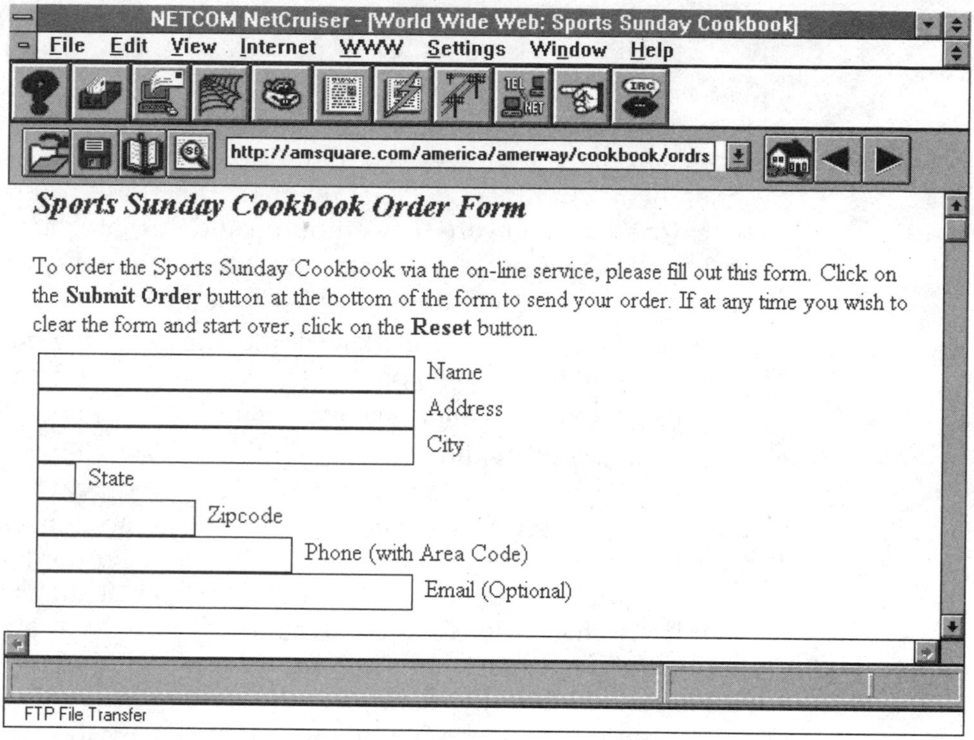

Figure 3-6. Made in America's fill-in-the-blank order form.

Name

Mailing address

Phone number

Fax number (optional)

E-mail address (optional)

Credit card preference (American Express, Visa, MasterCard, etc.)

Credit card number

Credit card expiration date

Quantity and name of products and/or services desired

Preferred method of shipping (i.e., UPS, Overnight Express, United States Postal Service)

Date of order

Other information (i.e., message on a gift card, size of a clothing item)

The information gathered through the use of such a form is usually automatically e-mailed directly to the storefront's owner's or manager's e-mail address, where it can be read like any other e-mail, and then processed like any other order for goods and/or services.

Caution: Data collected, such as credit card information, by a storefront operation and/or e-mailed via the Internet may not always be secure and free from the prying eyes of individuals who might use such information in an improper or illegal manner. Therefore, you should take a few extra steps to ensure the communication of information is secure. See Chap. 7, "Security Issues," for more information on protecting credit card information and other sensitive data.

Other uses for a fill-in-the-blank form include gathering information for a catalog mailing list, customer service surveys, requests for future mailings, and other similar business needs.

❑ *Credit card authorization* (optional): With a special software program, it is possible to have your storefront call up a credit card authorization service to first verify that the customer's bank account has sufficient funds to cover the cost of the purchase before the order form is actually e-mailed to the storefront owner or manager. If the customer's account has sufficient funds, the order form is processed. If the customer has insufficient funds, a special notation can be displayed on screen, or a more private message returned to the visitor via e-mail, advising that credit authorization could not be obtained and the order was not processed.

Text-Only Option

Some visitors may not have the computing power (i.e., a fast enough computer processor, color monitor, or modem) to view the graphical elements in your storefront. Therefore, it is recommended that you offer visitors a text-only display option. See Fig. 3-7.

How this option operates is simple. This feature is actually a Hypertext Link to a special page or pages where all your storefront information is listed in text format only, as menus and submenus. While traditional or conventional in display, and often seen as boring when compared to the more attractive graphical interfaces, it enables visitors who cannot read graphics to access your service.

Navigating Within Your Storefront

The preceding elements are primarily used to create the "look and feel" of your electronic storefront. While the Hypertext Link element can be used

Text-only option

Figure 3-7.   A text-only option.

as a major, if not *the* major, means of navigating (i.e., moving from page to page) within your storefront, the actual software program you elect to use to access the Web function of the Internet will also provide you with navigational controls.

Your copy of NetCruiser contains various functions to enable you to move from one page to another, to print information, to save information to disk, as well as to jump from your storefront to any other storefront on the Internet.

Elements to Avoid When Creating Your Storefront

While we recommend that first-time business owners and entrepreneurs use the indirect access option for connecting to the Internet, this type of access has one disadvantage: Transmitting data from your computer to the server computer and back takes more time than if you had a direct connection into the Internet. This disadvantage is also true for many of your storefront customers who elect to subscribe to an indirect access option with an Internet access service provider in order to reach the Internet.

Therefore, if you incorporate elements into your storefront that require long periods of download time (i.e., the time required for the elements to be transferred via modem from your customers' Internet access server computer to their personal computers), your customers may experience long delays as their computer screens wait to fill in the images and text.

To avoid or reduce this situation, it is strongly suggested that you avoid using the following elements:

❏ Animation sequences

❏ Large photographs and/or graphics

❏ Large sound clips

❏ Long video clips

These elements require a great deal of computer storage space and, as such, take much longer to transmit via modem than the other elements just discussed.

Since most people who use an indirect access option connect their computer to the Internet server computer via a 9600-, 14,400-, or 28,800-baud modem, this download issue will remain a factor until faster modems are installed.

Your storefront developer can help you determine which elements should not be included in your storefront.

Expand Your Offerings Without Increasing Your Cost

Logic would dictate that the more information and services you offer customers from your storefront location, the better those customers will be served, and the more they will refer new customers to your service. However, this is often difficult when a new business is starting up, or when you have limited staff with which to compile and create the many services needed to meet all your customers' needs.

As a means of offering customers more resources without having to create the resources yourself, and without having to spend a single cent, you may wish to consider creating a Hypertext Link between your storefront and other storefronts that provide the information and service you lack.

For example, assume your storefront was devoted to informing customers about bed and breakfast inns in New England. As a service to your customers, you might ordinarily provide information about various recreational services and tourist attractions in your community. To collect such information would take time and money. However, if another businessperson has already created such a storefront, it would be helpful to your customers to link your storefront to your colleague's recreational storefront. By doing so, your customers would benefit from increased information and service without your having to spend time and money to produce such an added benefit.

Your storefront developer can help you identify related services, and can make the link between your storefront and distant storefronts.

Branch Information Services, which has been offering Internet programming and consulting for over 11 years, has had a great response for their commercial services. The Branch Mall, the Internet's first and largest on-line electronic mall, arose out of their expertise over one year ago, and now boasts over 100 storefronts.

We could site numerous facts and figures about the Internet and its recent commercial activity, but while facts and figures speak loudly, we know from our own professional experience that the Internet is a great place to advertise and sell. We have been very impressed with the response both from companies requesting our catalog and also from on line Internet shoppers. As the developer and manager of the Branch Mall, we have seen the mall grow from six or seven storefronts in June 1994 to over one hundred storefronts in February 1995. The growth is exponential. Where once we were placing about one company online per week, we now are placing about three per week. This tremendous growth is coupled with a significant increase in consumer confidence and on line activity. We have seen the number of accesses to the Branch Mall grow at a great rate. Now averaging 15,000 accesses per day, and it continues to grow at 25 percent per month. The cycle of Internet growth and activity continues to grow as companies discover the advantages of advertising and as consumers become more secure with shopping on the Net. We constantly speak to individuals and companies who echo excitement of worldwide Internet marketing/shopping. Branch is committed to maintaining its premiere position as a mall and storefront developer utilizing high-speed servers, T3 speed Internet connections, and encryption technology.

John Zeeff
Branch Mall developer and manager
1-800-349-1748
branch-info@branch.com
http://branch.com/

Cautions:

❏ Obviously, It would not be wise to create a link to another storefront that offers the same services and/or information as you do. That would amount to sending your customers to another merchant. However, storefronts that offer related information would be ideal.

❏ Before creating such a link, contact the storefront to whom you wish to link and get the owner's agreement to link the storefront to yours. By doing so, your customer will have an easy means of returning to your place of business. It is easy for an Internet user to jump from one location to another and, once there, forget how to get back to the first location. By creating a return link, you reduce the chances of losing your customer.

Using Cybermalls to Spread the Word

Scattered throughout the Internet and becoming more and more popular each day are electronic shopping malls, often referred to as *cybermalls*. These malls are actually a special kind of storefront where information about various businesses and professional services (that have opened storefronts on the Internet) can be found.

For Internet shoppers, the use of cybermalls is quickly becoming an easy means of finding out which businesses and services are online, along with the addresses (URLs) for the businesses or services they wish to use. For business owners, cybermalls provide them with an easy and inexpensive way of advertising their storefronts to the masses.

Some malls charge a fee to have a business listed; others do not. See Chap. 10, "Cybermalls," for a sample list, with their URL addresses. Visit these malls, and select a number that you wish to use to increase the awareness of your own storefront.

Also use the Gopher function in NetCruiser to search the Internet for other cybermalls.

Recommended Internet Access Equipment

To access the Internet, your storefront, and other storefronts, certain computer equipment and software will be needed. At this point, when you ask whether an IBM or IBM-compatible versus an Apple Macintosh is better suited for accessing the Net, you may encounter some heated answers, depending on people's personal experiences and system preferences.

As experienced IBM and IBM-compatible users, with much less experience on Macintosh systems, our suggestions are biased by our experience. Our intention is not to insinuate that PC systems are better suited or that the proper Internet connection cannot be accomplished equally as well with a Macintosh based system. However, we have found more resources available for PC systems, as well as more people using PC systems to access and function on the Internet, than any other system. For these reasons, we have elected to provide information on PC equipment only. For readers who prefer a Macintosh system, we encourage you to speak to several Macintosh sales representatives to determine what kind of equipment would be appropriate.

To create a system that can be configured to provide you with an indirect access to the Internet, you should have the following items:

❏ *A 486 or faster computer:* While you can access the Internet with a 386 computer, speed is king. The faster you can communicate the more pleased you will be in the long run. A Pentium (or 586 class) computer is highly recommended.

❏ *8 or more megs of main memory:* 12 megs is better, and 16+ is best!

❏ *As large a hard disk as you can afford* (at least 300+ megs): While you may think less than 300 megs of free hard disk space will be sufficient, you'll soon learn how quickly you can fill a hard disk with software programs and data.

❏ *A 15 inch, .28 pitch, 256 color SVGA monitor, with 1 meg of memory on the video card.*

❏ *A 28,800 baud modem:* Either internal or external will do.

❏ *A 300 dpi or higher laser printer.*

❏ *A World Wide Web browser:* This is a software program used to access the Internet and its storefront locations. Your copy of NetCruiser provides this.

❏ *An Internet access service:* You'll need phone access to a service (computer) that has direct access to the Internet. NetCruiser provides this.

Storefront Design and Operational Considerations

At some point, you will need to discuss your storefront interests and plans with storefront developers if you are to successfully achieve your goals. Your task will be to convey to these individuals how you want your storefront to look, how it should function and operate, what kind of information and data should be posted online, and other operational considerations. Do not expect the developers to design your storefront for you; their job is to advise as to what is possible, and then to take your design decisions and turn them into reality.

Before designing your own storefront, it would be wise to surf the Internet and view other storefronts; see, for example, our sample storefronts located throughout this book. Determine what you like and do not like about these existing storefronts. Record the URL address of every storefront you visit that has a feature you like or do not like. Ask your storefront developer to examine the storefronts on your list to better understand what you want in your own storefront.

The more information you are able to share with the developer regarding your objectives and preferences, the more likely your storefront will meet your expectations.

Caution: Once a storefront is developed, redesigning can become very costly in terms of time and money. It is imperative that you first carefully lay out a design plan before any programmer begins working. Your storefront is actually nothing more than computer code written by a computer programmer. Depending on the design and content of your storefront, the amount of code necessary to build your storefront could be substantial. Considering the fees charged today by talented programmers (sometimes exceeding $100 or $200 per hour), you could run up a very large fee if you decide after the fact to redesign your storefront because you don't like the way the first design looks or functions.

The best way to avoid this common problem is to prepare answers to as many of the questions in Fig. 3-8 as possible. These are the questions that most storefront developers would ask of you when attempting to understand what kind of storefront you wish to build. It is not anticipated that you can answer all the questions; some can be answered only by the developer. However, using the Storefront Planning Worksheet in App. B, answer as many as possible, and then plan to review all of them with your developer.

Hypertext Markup Language (HTML) Editor

When you visit a storefront, the text you see on screen has been prepared for on screen display using a special software program called a hypertext markup language (HTML) editor.

Similar in function and use to a word processing program, information is keyed into an HTML editor. The program then encrypts the text with special codes to determine where text and graphic information should be positioned on screen. It is these codes that a Web browser (such as NetCruiser) reads to display the text and graphic information you see on your screen.

Producing HTML documents is not a difficult task, and anyone with a little training can learn how to use an HTML editor.

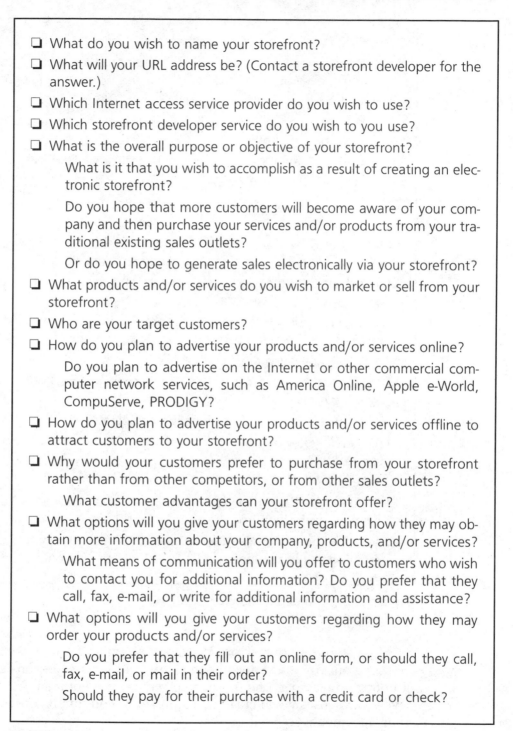

❑ What do you wish to name your storefront?

❑ What will your URL address be? (Contact a storefront developer for the answer.)

❑ Which Internet access service provider do you wish to use?

❑ Which storefront developer service do you wish to you use?

❑ What is the overall purpose or objective of your storefront?

What is it that you wish to accomplish as a result of creating an electronic storefront?

Do you hope that more customers will become aware of your company and then purchase your services and/or products from your traditional existing sales outlets?

Or do you hope to generate sales electronically via your storefront?

❑ What products and/or services do you wish to market or sell from your storefront?

❑ Who are your target customers?

❑ How do you plan to advertise your products and/or services online?

Do you plan to advertise on the Internet or other commercial computer network services, such as America Online, Apple e-World, CompuServe, PRODIGY?

❑ How do you plan to advertise your products and/or services offline to attract customers to your storefront?

❑ Why would your customers prefer to purchase from your storefront rather than from other competitors, or from other sales outlets?

What customer advantages can your storefront offer?

❑ What options will you give your customers regarding how they may obtain more information about your company, products, and/or services?

What means of communication will you offer to customers who wish to contact you for additional information? Do you prefer that they call, fax, e-mail, or write for additional information and assistance?

❑ What options will you give your customers regarding how they may order your products and/or services?

Do you prefer that they fill out an online form, or should they call, fax, e-mail, or mail in their order?

Should they pay for their purchase with a credit card or check?

Figure 3-8.   Storefront checklist.

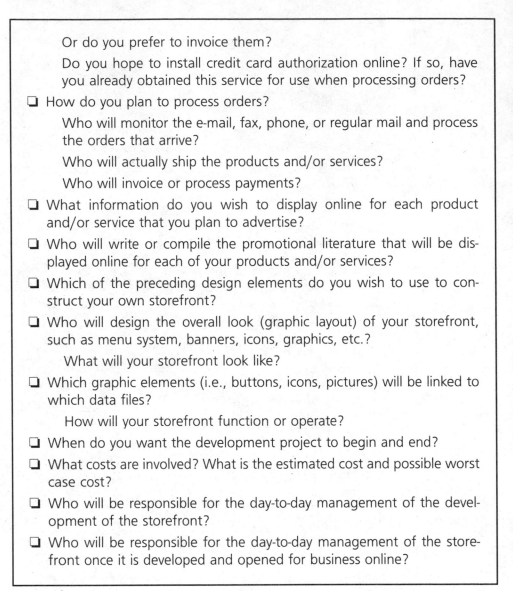

Or do you prefer to invoice them?

Do you hope to install credit card authorization online? If so, have you already obtained this service for use when processing orders?

❏ How do you plan to process orders?

Who will monitor the e-mail, fax, phone, or regular mail and process the orders that arrive?

Who will actually ship the products and/or services?

Who will invoice or process payments?

❏ What information do you wish to display online for each product and/or service that you plan to advertise?

❏ Who will write or compile the promotional literature that will be displayed online for each of your products and/or services?

❏ Which of the preceding design elements do you wish to use to construct your own storefront?

❏ Who will design the overall look (graphic layout) of your storefront, such as menu system, banners, icons, graphics, etc.?

What will your storefront look like?

❏ Which graphic elements (i.e., buttons, icons, pictures) will be linked to which data files?

How will your storefront function or operate?

❏ When do you want the development project to begin and end?

❏ What costs are involved? What is the estimated cost and possible worst case cost?

❏ Who will be responsible for the day-to-day management of the development of the storefront?

❏ Who will be responsible for the day-to-day management of the storefront once it is developed and opened for business online?

Figure 3-8. Storefront checklist *(cont.)*.

As a storefront owner, one decision you will have to make is who will prepare your hypertext documents? This could be the responsibility of the storefront developer, one of your employees, or yourself. If you wish to save on expenses when creating a storefront, you might consider creating your documents yourself.

While any text editor could be used to create hypertext documents, it is preferable to use a program created specifically for this purpose. Fortunately, there are a number of free HTML editors available for downloading from the Internet. Check App. C, "Internet Resource Directory," for information about other HTML editors. One popular program can be obtained by accessing the following URL address:

http://www.ncsa.uiuc.edu/General/Internet/WWW/HTML Primer.htm1

Remember: Case is important in URL addresses; so enter this address exactly as written.

Usage Statistics: Get the Facts

Like any other sales outlet, you should determine how effective your storefront is in terms of generating new sales or sales inquiries. One measure of the value of your storefront is to determine how many people actually visit it on a daily, weekly, and monthly basis.

This information is usually obtained from the Internet access service provider with whom you have contracted to connect to the Internet. Ask your storefront developer to provide you with regular reports indicating its use.

If the first month on the web is any indication of how good or bad a commercial venture is going to be, I would say that things are looking pretty good. After doing Web policy for Department of Defense and setting up a few servers, I figured I would try it myself. Our first venture was a cruise-only travel agency known as CRUISIN. There is no (physical) storefront, so all business is derived from the WWW. Our server is somewhat unknown, but people are beginning to bump into it on a regular basis. We had our first customer within 12 hours of loading the HTML code. There was nothing for a couple days after that. We are now up to about one serious inquiry every day with sales on just under half.

Robert Longley
CRUISIN
1-800-MYSAILS
http://www.crocker.com/cruisin

While it is not always possible to determine which specific services and/or products each visitor accessed, and how often they were accessed, while navigating within your storefront, you should be able to obtain information regarding how many people called up your storefront, during which days of the week, and during which hours of the day. Understanding the traffic pattern of your storefront will provide clues to how it can best be utilized by your customers.

Another method of determining the amount of use your storefront receives is to code your orders to identify them as coming from your storefront. For example, if you offer hand-painted sweatshirts for sale, you could assign a unique stock number to each item to identify it as being purchased from your storefront, especially if your sweatshirts are available from other sales outlets. Then when orders arrive at your actual place of business, you can quickly identify the orders that were generated from your electronic storefront.

Whichever method you prefer, collect as much data as possible on the use of your storefront, as such information can be helpful when planning the future of your business.

Customer Feedback

There is no more valuable information to the long-range success of your storefront than feedback from customers. If given the opportunity, your customers will tell you what is right and wrong with your business. All too often, business owners shy away from soliciting negative information from customers. However, this very information contains the clues to how you can increase your success in the future. To correct what's wrong, you first need to know what's wrong. Correct your faults and what you have left is a smooth running and satisfactory service.

One easy means of gathering feedback from customers is to include a Customer Feedback form somewhere within your storefront, a form on which customers can express their feelings, leave constructive criticism or words of praise, ask questions, and furnish other related information. Such a form could either be a:

❏ Free flowing statement, i.e., customers enter whatever information they wish.

❏ Fill-in-the-blank form, i.e., from a list of specific questions, customers are asked to type in answers.

❏ Checklist, i.e., from a list of specific statements or questions, each with a selection of answers, customers are asked to choose an answer option or options, such as yes, no, uncertain, true, false, pleased, displeased, etc.

Whenever the information is entered and the customer selects a special button labeled Completed or Quit, the information is then e-mailed to you for your review and response. Your storefront developer can help you design a customer service function that suits your needs.

Future Expansion Plans

It may seem premature to start thinking about how you might expand your electronic storefront, considering you have yet to build it, but understanding how a storefront can grow can help you more effectively plan its early design.

There are four common ways to expand your storefront business. You could:

1. Add more products and/or services that your company now offers, or plans to offer in the future, to your existing storefront.
2. Act as a "sales representative" for other products and/or services offered by other companies, by marketing those products and/or services in your storefront.
3. Create different storefronts for marketing and selling a completely different line of products and/or services than what you now offer.
4. Create an electronic mall, whereby other companies can set up shop at your location to promote their products and/or services.

The Internet represents one additional way of marketing my business to the public. Bogen's has received additional business as a result of its placement on the Net. We have a coupon on our home page, and have had several dozen coupons redeemed in the four months we have been listed. As with any business that tries to take advantage of new developments in technology, perhaps it is in anticipation of what might be around the corner that we look forward to most eagerly and are afraid to miss out on.

Bill Ellenbogen
Bogen's Restaurant
Blacksburg, Virginia
703-953-2233
http://www.biznet.com.blacksburg.va.us/~bogens/

Growth and diversity are important factors in the long-range success of any business. Since you can create as many pages and menu structures as you wish, the growth of your storefront, at least in theory, is unlimited. Perhaps one of the best means of understanding how your storefront can be expanded is to visit as many storefronts as you can on the Internet.

One of the advantages of traveling on the Internet is you can visit stores all over the country and across the globe in only a matter of seconds, without leaving the comfort of your computer chair. Set aside some time each month to surf the Internet, locate new storefronts, see how others have set up their businesses, and you'll find clues as to how you can improve your storefront.

4

To Market,
to Market ...

by Rob Kost

As with all business ventures, whether established in a traditional office location or offered electronically on the Internet, foremost for success has to be the marketing plan, as designed and implemented by the business owner. You will make a fatal error if you expect that all you have to do to generate profit on the Internet is to set up a storefront. Marketing your storefront, both on and off the Internet, will be necessary.

Considering the unique, and sometimes restrictive, nature of the Internet culture or community, you can make a second fatal error by advertising your storefront by simply sending out unlimited e-mail notices to everyone you find who's online, announcing you're open for business. This will result in widespread and immediate "punishment" by the many members who detest the use of the Internet for commercial gain. However, there are correct ways of using the Internet to advertise your business.

All storefront owners would be wise to carefully follow the advice presented in this chapter by Rob Kost. Rob is one of today's hot all-stars in this new and emerging industry. As a member of the Internet Development Group for PRODIGY, Rob has the unique understanding of the Internet community, its rules regarding personal and commercial behavior, and how the business objectives of storefront owners can best be achieved. The opportunities for creating profit are here now, but can be achieved only if you first understand the realities of the Internet community.

Introduction

If you're reading this, you've already heard much of the hyperbole about the Internet, how it is the publishing phenomenon of the nineties, and how it promises to transform commerce into the next millennium. You may even be a "net surfer" yourself.

You've heard that over half of the Fortune 500 are currently on the Net, and have seen statistics attesting to phenomenal growth. You've heard about the popularity of the World Wide Web (referred to as the Web or WWW), currently at about 37,000 sites, and are no doubt aware of efforts to bring commerce to the Web by providing for the secure transmission of sensitive information (like credit cards). For example, NetScape Communications, a leading publisher of software for use in navigating the Internet, already offers a secure client/server environment, and many others are working on various forms of secure electronic payment systems.

Ebullient reviews of the business potentials exist, typically published by those in the business of establishing sites for other businesses. Take, for example, the following description of the advantages of Internet for business from The Internet Group (http://www.tig.com):

> Businesses are finding the Internet to be an extremely cost-effective utility for reaching new customers and for obtaining reliable product, research, market, and service information in support of their business endeavors. The advantages that may be gained by business using the Internet are so significant that many industry leaders consider Internet usage to be key to a business's future viability. Statements such as "If you're not an active Internet citizen by the mid 1990's, you're likely to be out of business by the year 2000" made by Patricia Seybold [who is an author on the subject of doing business on the Net] emphasize the experts' belief that the Internet is a critical component of any business's long-term survival.

Yet the ability to conduct commerce is a necessary, but not sufficient, condition for actually making sales. "Selling" in this sense requires more than just the technical ability to receive payment. It requires the ability to market a product or service, and all that that entails: determining a target market and its needs for your product or service, and then finding a way to communicate the benefits that this target market will obtain from the purchase of your goods or services (or, put plainly, advertising).

Precisely what constitutes "marketing" in this new environment remains one of the least understood challenges to a business seeking to use the Internet as a channel for sales. While a definitive answer to this question is unlikely to emerge for some time (the players and the technology of the Web will likely not stabilize anytime soon), it is possible to describe some general strategies that businesses can use (and have used) to address the issue of how to market on the Internet.

The Internet was not built with commerce in mind; it was built by scientists for publishing and sharing information. These purposes were not afterthoughts; they were built into the very architecture of the system. Though tempting, metaphors such as "malls," "billboard advertising," "strategic location," and other items of parlance in the physical world have very little meaning in the context of a flat, networked environment. The lack of traditional metaphors and signposts is not merely a temporary inconvenience on the way to the "reestablishment" of conventional marketing approaches; it imposes a requirement that the question "what is marketing" be reconsidered entirely.

This chapter describes the problems presented to the marketer, which to this author represent the failure of traditional mass marketing methods, and suggests strategies for alternative methods of marketing in this new marketplace. Though examples in this chapter tend to dwell on retailing, the principles can be applied equally well to the world of business-to-business marketing and sales as well.

A Statement of the Problem

If by "marketing" we mean the ability to understand a market (its size, demographics, and needs), to position and price our product against the competition, and to identify prospects and communicate effectively with them, then the marketer on the Internet is faced immediately with several problems: ignorance, passivity, and blindness.

Ignorance

Very little is known about the users that make up the Internet. There exist no reliable estimates of the total size of the universe or its constituents. The most often quoted measurement of Internet size, published by the Internet Society, is derived primarily from the number of host computers that are on the net: As of January 1995, 4.8 million host computers (computers actually forming part of the Internet), representing a growth of 26 percent for the fourth quarter of 1994. Extrapolating the number of users from the number of hosts is tricky business. Is it 10 users per host? If so, the number of users has ballooned to 48 million from a similar estimate of 30 million made in July of 1994.

A different estimate from Matrix Information and Directory Services (http://www.tic.com), based on a survey made in October of 1994, holds that 7.8 million entities provide some form of interactive service (e.g., TELNET, Gopher, WWW) Internet access, 13.5 million users of such interactive services, and 27.5 million users that have access to electronic e-mail via the Internet.

FIND/SVP, in telephone surveys of consumers, concludes that approximately 3 million "consumers" currently use the Internet, making Internet consumer penetration larger than any of the "big three" online services (America Online, CompuServe, or PRODIGY). However, the same study concludes that the bulk of consumers accessing the Internet—about 2 million—do so through the online services. Furthermore, the primary use that these consumers make of the Internet is electronic mail, meaning that the World Wide Web is really accessible to no more than 1 million consumers as of the time of the FIND/SVP study.

These statistics are changing extremely rapidly. PRODIGY introduced its Web Browser in January of 1995, and within the first few weeks added over 250,000 new "Web consumers." America Online and CompuServe are expected to follow suit later this year, and a host of other smaller, consumer-oriented services such as Pipeline will also bring their share of consumers to the Web. It is relatively safe to say that, by year-end 1995, well over 3 million consumers had access to the Web.

If the only reliable statement concerning total size of the Internet (and particularly the Web) universe is that it is "large" and "getting larger," what can be said about the demographic make-up of that universe? In other words, what can we conclude about the needs of this undetermined market? What, in other words, sells? As might be expected, the answer is "even less." One study (based on self-selected samples) concluded that 95 percent of the users are males between the ages of 22 and 30, i.e., college students and engineers. Any number of studies are currently underway to refine these figures. The addition of online service users will, of course, skew these figures enormously (and probably favorably).

Passivity

Is it not enough to say that the size of the universe is large and getting larger? Perhaps it is not important to know in detail the "who" and "how many" that drive traditional business cases. After all, the costs of connecting to the network are relatively minuscule. Depending on capacity requirements, a presence on the World Wide Web might cost between $5000 and $50,000, with monthly costs between $700 and $2500—a pittance compared to the costs of a physical storefront and employees to populate it.

The real problem comes with attempts to inform the unknown populace of one's existence and product. The options that exist today for active transmission of information—electronic e-mail and bulletin boards (referred to as Newsgroups)—are absolutely intolerant of unsolicited commercial information. The 1994 case of the Arizona lawyers offering "green card" services through Newsgroups proved a valuable object lesson in Internet culture. In the words of The Internet Group, the lesson is as follows:

> For the business professional, the meaning of this is clear and absolute—products and information cannot be advertised in a broadcast manner or overtly requested. Unsolicited sales pitches of any form and blatant self promotion are not tolerated. Transgressions of this nature will unquestionably cause the user community to retaliate in force. Violators of this unwritten rule will be "flamed." (Flaming is the process through which the guilty party could receive thousands of unwanted e-mail messages condemning the offending action.) The sheer volume of mail that could be received would likely render the user's network node incapable of handling the load and would prevent the transgressor from conducting meaningful business through the Internet. A boycott of the company's products, services, and interaction by way of the Internet with its employees could also occur. Although unlikely, cases have been documented of malicious intent directed toward the guilty party in the form of personal harassment with 2:00 a.m. home phone calls, as well as unwanted pager beeps and business phone calls.

If direct marketing approaches don't work in this new environment, is there nevertheless a way to mass market one's product or service? Is there a corollary to taking out a 30-second spot on the radio or a half-page ad in a newspaper?

The answer is probably "not yet." Some, like the online version of *Wired* magazine called *Hotwired,* have experimented with selling ad space as part of their online publication. A sponsor's image and hyperlink are embedded in the editorial in the hopes not only that brand image will be enhanced, but that users will actually navigate to the sponsor's site and make a purchase. Furthermore, there exist over a hundred Internet malls, which list categorically the links to World Wide Web storefronts, providing, in some cases, an easy way for shoppers who know what they want, to perhaps find products or services to meet their needs.

Any results that these publications and malls have achieved are, of course, proprietary (and the lack of secure transactions seriously skews conclusions that might be drawn from these results). It is important to note, however, that PRODIGY, which provides for secure transactions, which took merchandising and advertising as the foundation of its early business model, and which experimented with both an advertising-based editorial and a online mall approach, changed its revenue model when it became clear that its members were far more interested in communications and interactivity than in shopping online. In some cases—flowers and software, for example—results were extremely encouraging. The positive results were due, however, not primarily to the ability of merchants to advertise on the system, but to the fact that users viewed the ordering capability as a useful utility for obtaining what are, after all, tangible goods.

While there are many diagnoses for the failure of online shopping to live up to its expectations (user interface, lack of pictures, cumbersome ordering process, inability to accept cash, etc.), the fundamental observations that one comes away with are:

❏ *Culture lag:* "That's just not the way I do my (grocery, clothing, vacation, etc.) shopping."

❏ *Medium mismatch:* "That's not what I came here for."

❏ *Obscurity:* "I didn't know that was there—I saw only what I wanted to see."

❏ *Vendor-based (rather than product-based) sales:* "I wanted a VCR; I didn't want to visit ten different stores."

While many might seek to contrast PRODIGY's early experience with the World Wide Web, the lessons of this early pioneer in online commerce are instructive and cautionary. Compared to traditional media like newspapers, television, and radio, which are in many cases predicated on the existence of paid-for commercial messages, *the Internet seems a relatively passive marketing medium. You hang out your shingle, and hope that passers-by will drop in.*

Blindness

If we get past the issues of ignorance and passivity, what can be said about results-based, feedback-based marketing? In other words, is it not sufficient to learn and improve one's Internet-based marketing approaches based on experience, however limited? Can I not change and adapt my marketing, my product selection, and my advertising based on the feedback I get from visitors to my site? The kinds of questions you might like to have answered from usage information might include:

❏ Age and gender of the user.

❏ How they heard of your site.

❏ What were they seeking, whether they found it.

❏ Why did/didn't they buy?

Here again, Internet poses difficulties for the savvy marketer. Aside from information volunteered by the users (see the discussion of list development later in this chapter), very little can be known about customers that one is able to acquire. Unlike PRODIGY or even bulletin board systems, usage is machine-based rather than user-based. Usage reports generated by Web servers are cryptic, but exhaustive lists of server locations hitting your site, organized by domain name and file names accessed, and a total number of server hits by day or week. There is no information whatsoever concerning the users themselves, and precious little direct information with which to fine-tune a marketing approach.

Strategies for Net-Based Selling

This chapter may have ended with the preceding section, the conclusion being that the Internet is not only a difficult environment for the marketer, but also an impossible and even hostile environment for the business seeking to market its goods or services.

However, this is not the conclusion of this chapter. The Internet, as currently designed and as it will be improved on in the near future, provides an unprecedented, valuable and potentially profitable marketing medium, if the marketer is ready to rethink what marketing means in this new environment.

This counterintuitive conclusion is based on having a clear understanding of what it means to be in a network, in the broadest sense of the word. The Webster's definition that most appropriately fits is "an interconnected or interrelated chain, group or system." The marketer that views its product or service as an isolated, independent, self-sufficient item that exists separately from a context is bound for failure. Correlatively, the marketer that views its product or service as a valuable part of a larger whole, and its customers as relationships rather than "targets," may find the Internet a happy medium.

To comprehend this, we must first understand how users come to the Internet and make their way through it.

The Two Kinds of Net Customers

A useful, if oversimplified, taxonomy of Internet users is that of hunters versus grazers. As with all simplifications, this distinction has to be qualified with the word "sometimes." One may sometimes come to the Net in one capacity or the other, and one's actual usage may in fact be a blend of the two. Nevertheless, an understanding of this basic dynamic is necessary to provide appropriate marketing approaches.

Hunters

Hunters come to the Internet with a relatively specific purpose, seeking relatively specific information. This purpose may not be (and indeed is probably not) overtly commercial; that is, while hunters are after something specific, they may not have the specific intention of purchasing something or even seeing commercial messages. Instead, hunters want, ideally, to solve a problem or to accomplish a task. It's the difference between wanting to put a hole in the wall and wanting to buy a drill. The problem is the former; the solution (which you are offering) is the latter. For example:

❏ "I'm traveling to Europe in the spring, and want to know what to bring with me."
❏ "I want to know about living wills, and whether they're for me."
❏ "I want to know whether this medicine is safe to take with aspirin."
❏ "I enjoy music on compact disk. I wonder what's on the Web related to them?"

Hunters on the Internet today may use any one of several search engines, such as The World Wide Web Worm, Lycos, Web Crawler, or Yahoo. The results that they obtain typically look something like the data shown in Fig. 4-1. This search was done using Yahoo and the search words "compact" and "disc." The underlined items indicate links to either Web sites or other Internet locations.

Grazers

In contrast to hunters, grazers are on the Web for play and diversion. Grazers are motivated by a search for novelty and interest (and, with 1500 to 2000 new Web sites every month, there is much novelty to be found). Grazers move from link to link, using Hypertext as a sort of free association medium, occasionally finding something of direct interest and adding it to his or her "hotlist" or "bookmark" function for quick recall at a later time. The hotlist then becomes a new point of entry the next time the grazer comes to the Net. In all, grazers probably spend, on average, about 20 minutes a day meandering around the Net. Fed by novelty, grazers' activities on the Web peak during their first month or so, and lapse into occasional use thereafter.

Yahoo Search
[Yahoo | Up | Search | Mail | Add | Help]
8 matches were found containing all of the substrings (compact, disc).
Business:Corporations:Computers:Media
• Compact Disc Authoring - cheap Compact Disc authoring facility for one-off or small volume production of CD-ROMS
Business:Corporations:Music:CDs, Records, and Tapes
• Compact Disc Europe
• Compact Disc Music Clubs (BMG & Columbia House)
Business:Corporations:Music:CDs, Records, and Tapes:Compact Disc Connection
• Compact Disc Connection
• Compact Disc Connection Browsing and Ordering
• Compact Disc Connection FTP Server
Computers:Multimedia
• Compact Disc Formats
Other Search Engines
[Lycos | WebCrawler | EINet Galaxy | Aliweb | CUSI Search Engines | More...]
yahoo@akebono.stanford.edu
Copyright © 1995 David Filo and Jerry Yang

Figure 4-1.   Yahoo search data.

Find Your Place in the Matrix

Your task, as a marketer in a web of hunters and grazers, is to strategically place references to your site in a way that gathers in both types of users. There are at present only a few methods of doing this.

Hunters

The most straightforward way to gather in the hunters is to ensure that information about your storefront is included in at least one of the many search engines (also referred to as "agents," "spiders," or "webcrawlers") available on the Web. These search engines traverse the Web, looking for descriptive information embedded in pages and building indices to URLs (storefronts). Searches produce lists of hits, ranked by relevance, and typically contain the text that produced the hit in the first place. Some indices, such as that provided by EINet Galaxy (http://www.einet.net/), add human editors to the otherwise automated task of compiling sites. The Global Network Navigator, offered by O'Reilly and Associates, also compiles a What's New list that is updated weekly. Formerly sited at the National Center for Supercomputing Applications, the What's New list can now be found at http://nearnet.gnn.com/gnn/wn/whats-new.html). In many cases, you can add your storefront's description directly into the search engine in question (for example, Yahoo has a form to solicit a self-description {http://akebono.stanford.edu/yahoo/}, as does Lycos {http://lycos.cs.cmu.edu/}).

Relying on the capabilities of a search engine to describe your site, it behooves you to construct your documents in as fully self-describing a way as possible. In particular, pay attention to the information contained within the header HTML tag. This tag, symbolized as <HEAD>, contains subelements such as TITLE, BASE, ISINDEX, LINK, and META that are often keys for search engines.

If you manually enter information about your site into a search engine's index, be as descriptive and accurate as possible. If, for example, your site is selling compact disks, use alternative spellings ("disk" and "disc"), and words that are properly associated with the subject (including, for example, "music," "classical," "jazz," "rock," "audio," "stereo," "stereophonic," etc.).

Grazers

Grazers are a bit more difficult to gather in. Two principal methods may prove fruitful. One relates to a theory (of mine) that the Web will tend to coalesce around "gravitational centers of interest." That is, users of like interest will tend to navigate to sites that contain like content. *To avail yourself of this gravitational pull, you may want to construct intersite linkage agreements.* To understand the importance of your cooperation with other sites, recall our definition of network: "an interconnected or interrelated chain, group or system." If you are selling CDs, you may want to agree with other sites that specialize in music to include cross-linkages between your site and theirs. The agreement need not be a formal one, and might even be (and often is) done spontaneously. Even erstwhile competitors (i.e., other sellers of compact disks) should consider such cross-linkages (users will likely find both of your sites anyway, and in a networked environment, competitiveness lies not in hiding information, but in being the best provider of service and content).

In seeking out grazers, you should also consider participation in Newsgroups. There exist about 8000 such bulletin board discussion groups across the Internet, focused on very specific subjects. Find one of relevance to your business and participate. Here, for example, is a list of Newsgroups of potential relevance to the seller of CDs:

- ❏ alt.music.alternative
- ❏ alt.music.alternative.female
- ❏ alt.music.amy-grant
- ❏ alt.music.awk-jam
- ❏ alt.music.bela-fleck
- ❏ alt.music.billy-joel
- ❏ alt.music.blues-traveler
- ❏ alt.music.canada
- ❏ alt.music.complex-arrang
- ❏ alt.music.deep-purple
- ❏ alt.music.dream-theater
- ❏ alt.music.ecto
- ❏ alt.music.elo
- ❏ alt.music.enya
- ❏ alt.music.filk
- ❏ alt.music.france
- ❏ alt.music.from.the.hearts.of.alt.config
- ❏ alt.music.gwar
- ❏ alt.music.hardcore
- ❏ alt.music.james-taylor
- ❏ alt.music.jethro-tull
- ❏ alt.music.jewish
- ❏ alt.music.kylie-minogue
- ❏ alt.music.led-zeppelin
- ❏ alt.music.les-moore
- ❏ alt.music.marillion
- ❏ alt.music.misc
- ❏ alt.music.monkees
- ❏ alt.music.moody-blues
- ❏ alt.music.nin
- ❏ alt.music.nirvana

- alt.music.pat-mccurdy
- alt.music.pearl-jam
- alt.music.perl-jam
- alt.music.peter-gabriel
- alt.music.pink-floyd
- alt.music.prince
- alt.music.progressive
- alt.music.queen
- alt.music.roger-waters
- alt.music.rush
- alt.music.sed-jam
- alt.music.ska
- alt.music.smash-pumpkins
- alt.music.sonic-youth
- alt.music.swedish-pop
- alt.music.synthpop
- alt.music.techno
- alt.music.the-doors
- alt.music.tmbg
- alt.music.todd-rundgren
- alt.music.u2
- alt.music.world

I stress the word "participate" because that is exactly what you must do. Overt selling and inattention to the context of the ongoing conversations will backfire, resulting in flames and boycotts. You must have something to bring to the conversation other than your offer to sell. Presumably, if you are in the business (of, e.g., music), you have knowledge and/or opinions that can benefit others in the group. It is not contrary to "netiquette" to sign your notes with your e-mail address and/or URL, but be cautious. Again, as The Internet Group has observed:

> The information presented by commercial (and all other) users must be of demonstrable value and interest. Direct solicitation of sales or the self-promotion of products and services will not be tolerated. Data related to products and services must be shrouded within an informational format. Listening to customer input regarding topics of interest (e.g., technology, product functionality, and needs) and responding with helpful advice and/or infor-

mation is an accepted means of Intermarketing. Suggestions may be made to customers regarding sources (on the net or elsewhere) where additional information and reference material may be obtained, but commercial enterprises may not broadcast advertisements or initiate an Internet dialogue with an "offer to sell."

Give First, Then Receive

Because the Internet began as, and in its very structure is predicated on, a way of sharing information, you must reorient yourself to a way of thinking about commerce that is not overtly or even primarily about withholding. Your site should reflect this ethic. Again, using the example of the CD seller, the site should, in addition to cataloging and selling compact disks, offer such free goodies as:

❑ Reviews.

❑ Music samples (copyright permitting).

❑ Discographies.

❑ "Inside" information (reviews with musicians, etc.).

❑ Even Bulletin Boards (still a young technology on the Web).

If altruism goes against your business instincts, consider the following benefits to such an approach:

❑ It generates traffic (and likely repeat traffic).

❑ It generates a "buzz" in e-mail and Newsgroups ("Check out this site ...").

❑ It generates good will.

❑ It creates interest and an informed buying public.

Remember, you are in a networked environment: The more links, visits and word of mouth you are able to create, the more sales you're likely to make.

No Matter What You're Selling, You're Selling Information

Historians like to label eras with characterizations such as The Industrial Age, The Space Age, and so on. It is said that we are living in The Information Age. Whether this is in fact true, and what it actually means is not, for the moment, important. What is important in this context is that all transactions—even for the purchase of hard goods—are transactions in information.

The buyer coming to your site will expect complete, accurate, and useful information related to your product or service and to your industry and company. This means that items must be well categorized and described (including pictures where appropriate). Background information related to their manufacture and use should be presented. Disclaimers, warranties, limitations on warranties, and other legal information should be included. Terms of sale must be explicit. Records related to the purchase should be complete and accurate (this means having a robust, auditable, backend system).

In addition to being complete, accurate, and useful, the information you provide should also be fresh. If users come to your site twice, they should ideally see something new upon the second entry. If your site is static for too long, you are unlikely to benefit from repeat traffic. Just how frequently you update information is, of course, a function of the type of product or service you are selling. If the product doesn't change frequently (or at all), the ancillary information (describe in the previous section) should. Daily change is not necessary, but weekly or monthly change is probably appropriate to gather in the grazer.

You should also feel free to offer to include your users in an electronic mailing list (referred to as a List Serv). Never add users to a mailing list unless they have volunteered, or unless it is part of the quid pro quo for gaining access to ancillary information. The information provided through mailings should be informative and concise. (Many users pay for the time it takes to receive your message; don't make this onerous or expensive.) Electronic junk mail leaves a bad impression with users, and is increasingly filtered by mailbots anyway. Users should always have a way to easily opt out of the mailing list (typically, a List Serv application allows for this by typing "UNSUBSCRIBE" in the body of a return mail message).

Relationships, Not "Targets"

Mass and direct marketers deal with prospects and customers en masse; a pool of individuals is treated as a collective target group, which typically yields a certain response rate when solicited. While these concepts still work for purposes of analysis and refinement of a set of needs and product set(s), they are inappropriate when applied directly to users in an interactive, two-way environment. Unlike all other media preceding it, the online environment permits users to talk back. Implicit in this two-way environment is a relationship, a give and take between you and your customers.

This means that blind solicitations that have no regard for user preferences are unlikely to work. Instead, a savvy Net marketer will use the interactive character of the Net to determine what customers want, and to respond to dissatisfactions and concerns directly. You should not only be ready for a considerable volume of user e-mail; you should actively solicit it. The capability of the Web to permit user-completed forms is a useful way of soliciting and structuring user feedback. Forms can provide very detailed information about user needs and characteristics, enabling you to better hone your offering.

But, in your construction of customer profiles, you must be extremely sensitive to matters related to privacy. Privacy is of great concern to all users of the Internet. If you create lists, either through overt solicitation to fill out a form or through the process of collecting sale information, users should be informed that their names will be added to the list. You should also inform users what will be done with the list: Will it be sold? Will it be used to generate mailings? Will it be revealed to any third party? Will it be used for analysis? The best and most Net-acceptable policy concerning the collection and use of user-provided information is to promise that it will not (barring a subpoena) be revealed to any third party. The lists you generate can become a valuable asset of your company, and should not be sold or given away lightly.

The Rest of the World

Those involved in the world of the Internet sometimes tend to forget that it is not the only—or yet even a significant medium—for the communication of ideas and information. Newspapers, magazines, television, and

The *American Employment Weekly* has been online on the Internet since July of 1994. Prior to going online, I was somewhat skeptical about a storefront on the Net as a vehicle to sell subscriptions to our employment publication. I am pleased to report, however, that decision to open the *American Employment Weekly* storefront has been both sound and profitable. I would recommend opening a storefront to any business that wants to grow.

Bill Scott
AMERICAN EMPLOYMENT WEEKLY
219-277-3408
http://branch.com/aew/aew.html

radio still form the primary means by which information is conveyed and product awareness is generated. As with the progression of these media throughout the twentieth century, new forms of communications do not entirely displace the old; instead, there is complimentarity from one medium to the next. *TV Guide* is a printed publication about an electronic medium. Books and records are advertised through magazines. We go to the newspaper to find what's playing in the movie theaters.

So it is with the Internet. The Internet will not displace traditional ways of advertising your product or service; the conventional media may form excellent vehicles for generating interest and awareness of your site. It is still early in the rise of social consciousness about the Internet to consider a *Yellow Pages* listing with your URL, but it is worth considering whether to advertise in such vehicles as *NetGuide* magazine, which are targeted directly to the user base that forms your likely online customers. Press releases, URL, or e-mail addresses on business cards, and information contained in your paper mail (bill stuffers, direct mail cards, etc.) should also be considered.

The day will come, of course, when a URL or e-mail address is a standard part of contact information provided in advertising—right next to the 800 number. For now, however, it is more likely to mystify than to inform users of mainstream media.

Conclusions

The seemingly oxymoronic phrase "marketing on the Internet" is a contradiction in terms to the degree that one tries to apply traditional approaches to this new environment. As we have observed, new approaches to marketing are not only beneficial; they are essential. Interestingly, this new approach to marketing results in a number of paradoxes:

❑ Selling is done by giving away.

❑ Altruism coincides with self-interest.

❑ You are distinguished from others to the degree that you are related to them.

❑ Competition often takes the form of cooperation.

The successful marketer is one who understands and utilizes these paradoxes to his advantage (and to the advantage of everyone else on the Internet).

See you on the Net!

5
Selling Overseas

Grant's Flowers was, we are told, the first business to go online on a commercial mall. We aren't millionaires, but I wouldn't want to give it up. Everyday we get some business from having our storefront on the Internet—some days are better than others.

The Internet is a great leveling field for business. The small business can compete with the large corporations because of the low cost of having an Electronic Storefront, and being able to reach millions of people.

We receive orders for flowers from all over the world—mostly the United States, with Canada running second, but the rest are from all over. We also have a storefront for our Exotic Flowers from Hawaii. Exotic Flowers gets a number of orders from Japan and other Pacific Rim countries as well as European countries. The furthest inquiry we have had came from the Ukraine.

Larry Grant
Grant's Flowers and Greenhouse
1-313-769-6055
http://florist.com/flowers/flowers.html

Considering the global reach made possible with an Internet connection, some of the customers who visit your storefront may—and most likely will—be from a foreign country. Having a storefront accessible by anyone located anywhere in the world creates special problems that require special preparation and resources with which to service this segment of your new customer base. To ignore these special situations may result in lost sales!

In this chapter we discuss some of the special situations associated with selling overseas, which you should consider prior to setting up shop on the Internet. Some of these situations can also apply if you plan to market your products and/or services only to U.S. citizens.

Language Barrier

While English is perhaps the most widely spoken and written language in the world, it will not be appropriate to some foreign visitors who read and speak another language. If you begin to experience a great deal of traffic from foreign lands, or if you wish to solicit such traffic, you should consider installing an alternate language option on your storefront's home page.

Given such an alternative, when foreign speaking individuals arrive at your home page, they see a list of alternate language options displayed and as written in various languages. Each option should be written in the language itself (i.e., the French display option is written in French, the Spanish display option is written in Spanish, and so on). For example:

Select this option for the English display.

(insert the above statement here written in French)

(insert the above statement here written in Spanish)

(insert the above statement here written in Italian)

By selecting the preferred option, a Hypertext Link takes your visitor to a specially prepared version (page) of your storefront where the text is written in the selected language.

Naturally, to provide such an option, you will need to find several individuals who can convert your English text into the languages you need. Check with the foreign language departments at your local schools and colleges, as they often can help you find someone who can translate your English text.

Time Zones

If you invite customers to call for additional information or support, or if you need to call customers, pay attention to the time zones in which they're located. The last thing you want to do is call customers at 3:00 p.m.

(your time), only to wake them up at 3:00 a.m. (their time) from a sound sleep to share your latest, greatest, supersale offer!

To avoid the reverse, it would be wise to include in your customer support area, information regarding the time zone in which your company is located.

Currency Exchange

The good old American dollar is not worth a dollar in every country; sometimes it's worth more, sometimes less. You should require that all payment be made in U.S. funds, to avoid a foreign or domestic bank imposing an exchange rate, which could result in your taking a loss on the sale. Another option is to invite customers to use a credit card, since the card processing system will (most likely) calculate the correct exchange amount in U.S. dollars.

Caution: Not all credit authorization services will accept credit cards from all foreign countries. Before offering a credit card payment option to customers, you should discuss this situation with the credit authorization service you use to fully understand the options available.

Shipping

While we often complain about how the U.S. Postal Service works, it is extremely efficient in terms of moving large volumes of mail when compared to some foreign postal services.

Before you set up shop, you should talk to various delivery services, such as the following, to understand what options you have when it comes to shipping goods around the world:

❑ United Parcel Service (UPS)
❑ United States Postal Service (USPS)
❑ Federal Express
❑ Airborne Express
❑ DHL

Customer Service

Being available to all customers to answer all questions is an admirable philosophy for any business, and an objective entrepreneurs should strive to achieve. However, you must be realistic in terms of how many customers you can personally speak to each day by phone or by other means. If your storefront becomes popular, you can expect the number of e-mail, phone, fax, and regular mail contacts to become substantial. Some of these contacts will be from foreign countries requiring you to restructure your business hours to meet their schedules. How you manage these unique customer support issues will determine the future success of your business.

If the volume increases to a taxing level, you should consider adopting any or all of the following options:

❑ Hire someone to handle your phone, fax, e-mail, and mail correspondence.

❑ Install a frequently asked questions (FAQ) option in your storefront (where visitors can view or download a collection of questions typically asked of you, with your answers).

❑ Install a voice mail system.

❑ Install a fax-back service (where information can be returned automatically to customers via fax).

❑ Hire a telephone answering service.

❑ Bring in a partner to share the workload.

Technical Support

If you are selling from your storefront computer software programs or equipment that requires phone-based technical support, you will need to consider how best to offer such support, considering the various time zones that you will encounter. For example, you may need to hire a technical support person who will work from 12 midnight to 8 a.m. (your time) to be available when customers call from overseas.

Illegal Merchandise

The U.S. government imposes restrictions on which merchandise can and cannot be sold overseas. Before you set up shop, contact the U.S. Department of Commerce in Washington, D.C., or speak with an experienced import-export consultant or lawyer, to determine if any restrictions exist on the merchandise you intend to sell overseas.

Importing-Exporting Regulations

Selling goods overseas is not as easy as packing up the goods in a secure mailing box and then shipping them to your distant customer. Right or wrong, the U.S. government has imposed a strict set of guidelines governing the goods that may be sold overseas, and how they must be packaged, shipped, and financed. These regulations can at times be confusing! It is recommended that you seek the assistance of an import-export consultant, even for a few hours, to learn more about how you should handle purchase orders from foreign customers, if you plan to market heavily to customers overseas.

A review of several books on the subject of importing-exporting would also be advisable in order to identify other issues that you should consider before opening up shop on the Internet. To obtain such information, check with your local libraries and commercial bookstores, as well as the U.S. Department of Commerce in Washington, D.C. (you may obtain their phone number from directory information).

Cultural Differences

While not always possible, it is advisable that you attempt to consider the differences in culture and custom between Americans and those of distant cultures. For example, here in America, it's considered courteous to ask a new customer about his health and the welfare of his family. Such questions as "How are you today?" or "How's the family?" are asked millions of times each day. Often this is done simply to break the ice and put the customer at ease, and the answers to such questions are often irrelevant. After all, the more familiar customers become with your business, the more comfortable they may feel, and therefore the more likely they may be to purchase from your service.

However, such delving into one's private life in some foreign countries is considered rude, boorish, and an invasion of the individual's private life. Before you set up shop with the world, it would be wise to review a few books dealing with the subject of cultural customs.

"Don't Know You from Adam" Syndrome

Since many of your customers will be calling in from distant lands, they will not automatically recognize your service or company—regardless of how big and successful your company is in the United States. As such, they may have questions regarding your company's history, ability to provide services and merchandise, return policies, customer support practices, and other such information.

To overcome their natural shyness and precautionary nature, it might be wise for you to incorporate several testimonial statements online from satisfied customers, a letter from your local Better Business Bureau, a list of references customers may contact at will, and a copy of your warranty or guarantee policies.

6
Legal Considerations

by Edward Frankel

Nothing is more frustrating and unfortunately at times more costly for you as a business owner, than to discover that certain individuals are using your products and/or services illegally. We are all aware that shoplifting is a major problem in our retail shopping centers, and we all pay the price for this crime in the form of higher ticket prices. Now that you're about to open your electronic storefront, the last thing you want to have to deal with is a law suit to stop someone from illegally using your hard earned property, and to compensate you for your lost revenue. But that's exactly what can happen in cyberspace if you fail to take a few precautions.

Before his untimely death, no one was better suited than Edward Frankel to guide storefront owners in protecting their property, as well as storefront visitors in understanding their rights concerning the use of property made available via a storefront.

Reading this chapter can save you time and money later on when you have to protect your merchandise.

Legal Considerations

Protecting the property represented by your electronic storefront is inherently different from protecting your bricks-and-mortar storefront, and yet it is the same.

While you may not have a parking lot in the front, in starting and operating an electronic storefront you are still dealing with proprietary interests. You are selling either goods or services. You are profiting from the fact that some stuff is yours, not the property of others. In this chapter we will introduce the realities involved, and help you keep what is yours *yours*!

What makes something property? Certain categories of things are called "property" in our society because that is the way we see them, and so we instructed our lawmakers to make it so. What we call trademarks are property. A nebulous thing called copyright is something that can be owned, and the law recognizes that ideas can sometimes be treated as secrets that can also be owned, and therefore also stolen.

We recognize big money in these vague things. Trademarks (the exclusive legal right to call certain things by certain names) regularly sell for billions of dollars. In fact, in building your electronic storefront, ultimately all you are doing is starting to build the value of the name and the manner of doing business represented by your activities. So you better make sure that you can use the name you choose! Choosing legal assistance is no different from choosing any other professional services. You have to know what you are looking for, and realize that you as the buyer have every right to be choosy and demanding. Don't expect something for nothing, but there is nothing wrong with being clear about what you want!

Figure out What You Have of Value

Depending on the nature of your business, its value is going to reside in different things. You want to be careful about the things that are valuable, not the easily replaceable assets. If you develop software, you want to make sure that you can retain control over the software, which may be the code itself, the name you sell the software under, and maybe other services that you sell with the software. So the first thing you do is conduct an inventory of what is of value in your business.

Make a list of what makes your business different. Intangible assets have replaced capital as the most valuable asset of most modern businesses. Intangible assets include inventions, original works of authorship and creation, proprietary data, confidential information and know-how, trademarks, and other forms of technologies, knowledge, and information owned or controlled by the business.

Many of these assets are protectable by the traditional intellectual property categories of copyrights, trademarks, trade secrets, and patents, but significant assets are not. Your company's competitive advantage in the marketplace can be described in terms of the value of your intangible assets, and the value of these properties is a function of their inherent usefulness, your company's ability to exploit them profitably, and the security of your company's control over the assets.

Choice and Management of Trademarks

Trademarks, servicemarks, and tradenames are among your businesses' most valuable assets. These names and marks represent your investment in marketing and product quality. Your trademarks are the difference between doing business anonymously or as a recognized force in the market. As a company grows and prospers, so does the value of its trademarks. Often the value of a company is largely a function of the value of its marks. When Ford Motor Company purchased Jaguar PLC in 1989, it paid $2.5 billion for a company that by standard valuations of its financial performance was worth one-fifth that amount. The balance of $2 billion was publicly attributed by Ford to be for the famed Jaguar trademark.

Proper trademark strategy is not accidental. Like all valuable business assets, trademarks must be carefully chosen, developed, and protected if your company is to retain control over an appreciating and critical business resource. It is critical that proper screening be conducted when adopting a new mark to select one that can be used without infringement on other companies' established trademarks and one that will be eligible for legal enforcement. After adoption, registration in the appropriate domestic and foreign jurisdictions is the next step. Proper use of trademarks requires in-house systems and procedures to ensure that correct notices of ownership are employed and to actively monitor for potential infringement by competitors and businesses in related fields and industries.

The Value of Business Labels:
Names, Tradenames, Trademarks

Every business uses various types of "names," names that are a particularly valuable asset. These names are the labels or the faces of the company and of its products or services; they identify the company to its customers, suppliers, and competitors. In a very real sense these labels *are* the business.

Indicators of Source and Quality

This notion of identity is such a fundamental factor of the modern commercial world that it is often taken for granted. The problem of counterfeit goods is not endemic in our world, although it does still occur. When a box of film has the Kodak mark on it, we do not think twice about the source of the goods or whether what is actually inside the film can is an unserviceable roll of celluloid being sold as Kodak film. Think about doing business in the world if you could not assume that things are what they are represented to be and that, prior to every transaction, you would have to inspect and verify the authenticity and quality of goods.

Reputation of Source

From the beginning of human society, craftspersons sought to identify their products with a distinctive symbol or mark. As crafts guilds developed, distinctive hallmarks were utilized to identify the association of the goods with members of the guilds, as a means of establishing genuine goods originating from a specified source.

Trademarks and tradenames allow consumers and other participants in the commercial world to trade without undue concern about confusion, mistake, and deception in the identity of goods.

Tradefame

Where a business is successful, goodwill about the company and its products and services follows. A business's goodwill is the currency of its relationship with customers and the marketplace. This business reputation is ultimately the value of tradenames and trademarks; the names and marks allow the goodwill to be exercised by the act of purchasing a product or service so identified.

Today's commerce is to a large extent a function of trademarks and tradenames. Advertising creates and reinforces consumer preferences for a certain product or service, and refreshes the consumer's recollection of the source of those goods through identification of the tradenames or marks that identify the products. People buy what they have come to prefer, and use trade labels to find those preferences.

While the secret Coca Cola formula is undoubtedly valuable, it is overshadowed by the phenomenal value of the Coke® and Coca Cola® trademarks throughout the world. Even if I somehow acquired the genuine Coca Cola formula, I still might very well have a difficult time selling cola drink under my own name. But if I could use the Coke trademark and related designs, and if the Coca Cola Company did not have the ability to prevent such use, I might well be successful selling my own formula.

As a product comes to be preferred by consumers, competitors are tempted to take advantage of the attributes of the features and labels that associate a successful product with its source. Names, colors, shapes, packaging, and manner of use are all features that may be appropriated or even parodied to associate a competitor's goods with that of the preference leader.

Commercial morality has long included the right of a merchant to protect its goodwill and tradefame, by enforcing some degree of monopoly on the attributes of products and labels that serve to identify the source of the products and services. By either intent or oversight, others may be prohibited from conducting their businesses in such a manner as to create confusion in the marketplace as to the identity or source of products or services.

What Are Marks and Names?

The name of the company itself, as it is used promotionally, is the company's tradename, which may or may not be the same as the company's legal name. The names of products and services are trademarks and servicemarks, respectively. A trademark must not be confused with a tradename, which identifies a company. Coke is a trademark of The Coca-Cola Company. The Coca-Cola Company is a trade name.

A trademark is a word (or several words), a name, a symbol (such as one or more letters or numbers, or a design), or any combination of these, used to identify the goods of a manufacturer or merchant and to distinguish them from those manufactured or sold by others. Some well-known trademarks are Kodak™, Velcro™, Lysol™, and Teflon™. It is important to remember that in the United States, the mere use of a trademark to identify and distinguish the goods of one company from those of another creates trademark rights. However, to obtain additional advantages most companies register their trademarks in the United States Patent and Trademark Office.

There are four general benefits to federal registration of trademarks.

1. Registration serves to put other potential users of the trademark on notice that the trademark is in use, and is claimed as the exclusive property of another business.

2. Registration also creates a presumption of ownership and of exclusive rights to use the trademark in commerce, should a controversy arise and the matter go to court.

3. In certain situations, depending on the facts of the case, the registration may be conclusive evidence of ownership and rights to exclusive use, thus making enforcement more certain, swift, and economical.

4. Finally, registration serves as a basis for foreign registrations of the trademarks, which given the present reality of the commercial world, is more often than not a necessity.

As identifiers, trademarks are also distinguished from generic names, which are the common descriptive name of the product that may be also identified by specific trademarks. For example, "spray insect repellent" is the generic name that goes with Off™.

The trademark also serves as a guarantee of consistency and quality, as well as an aid in advertising and selling the product. A trademark owner has the right to prevent others from using the owner's marks or a mark so similar that its use by another is likely to confuse or deceive.

As discussed, tradenames and trademarks are identifiers; they serve to distinguish one company from another, or one product or service from another. It follows, then, that the less descriptive names and marks are, the better they work. Apple Computer™ is an example of an excellent tradename and trademark (it is used for both) because what do apples have to do with computers? Apple is an example of an *arbitrary* mark, a word that has other meaning, but the application of which to the products or services in question is arbitrary and without any substantive informational value.

Another category of mark that is inherently even stronger than an arbitrary mark is exemplified by the mark and tradename Xerox®. "Xerox" has no meaning except as it has developed in conjunction with the corporation and technology associated with the word "Xerox." This is an example of a *coined* mark.

Next down on a scale for relative strengths for marks are *suggestive* marks, marks that suggest characteristics appropriate for the business and its commercial activities. These are what are typically most popular with both consumers and management, for the very good reason that they are often easiest to promote and remember. Digital Computers and Off for insect repellent are well-known examples. Suggestive marks are protectable under law, but are often the most difficult to select without running into problems with undue similarity to other marks and tradenames already in use in the market in question.

Marks that are *descriptive* of the goods or services are inherently weak, and they are difficult to protect and enforce against use by competitors. Such descriptive marks would be typified, as an example, by the hypothetical mark Super Natural for health food snack items.

Certain categories of names are generally prohibited from use as trademarks. Geographic place names generally cannot be registered or enforced as trademarks, unless they have acquired *secondary meaning.* Secondary meaning is proven by asserting that the trademark is literally famous, and is recognized by a significant proportion of the buying public as an identifier for a particular company's products.

Personal names are also problematic, because the courts are hesitant to prevent a second Mr. Smith from using his surname Smith to identify his golf clubs, even though another Smith may have been manufacturing "Smith" golf clubs for many years prior. An exception is where the mark has acquired the tradefame of general recognition within its market as a specific product coming from a specific source.

Another issue that cannot be ignored is the nature of the proposed trademark when used in foreign markets. This is a very pertinent point that has tripped up major businesses in the past. The anecdotes are legion about the American trademarks that rendered products essentially unmarketable because of translations or connotations that were repulsive or at least unhelpful. This includes not only names and words, but colors and designs as well.

Coming up with good names can test the abilities of anyone, professional consultants included. It can be a very difficult task. Choosing a trademark is often the responsibility of a company's advertising staff or the department with the new product. In start-up companies this is most often the founders. Whatever the source of the mark, proper screening and investigation of the mark's potential protection must be considered prior to an investment through use. The specific steps that may be taken to minimize the risk in choosing new marks follow.

The Basis for Control over Marks and Tradenames: How Ownership Originates

In the United States, the first to make use of a trademark or tradename generally is the owner of that mark or name. As the owner, the first user has the right to exclude others from making use not only of the exact mark or name, but also of derivatives that might be confusingly similar.

When the origins of trademark law are kept in mind, this makes sense. The foundations of trademark law are social concerns about deceptive business practices and unfair competition: That to allow consumers to be confused about the source and identity of goods and services is to undermine the mercantile system itself. To the extent that trademark law clarifies which businesses have control over distinctive names, tremendous uncertainty is avoided in the buying and selling of the marketplace.

The *first in use–first in right* rule throws the burden on the company choosing new trademarks and business names to exercise diligence in choosing names that do not infringe the already existing rights of other companies.

Proper Label Management: Useful Procedures for Choosing and Protecting Trademarks

If there is one universal truth in the business world, it is this—never ever invest nickel one in a tradename or trademark before there is some assurance that it can be both:

❑ Used without infringing another name or mark.

❑ And protected against infringement by others.

An incredible amount of effort, time, and money has been wasted by businesses that, ignoring this rule, advertised and shipped product before learning that the names or marks could not be used.

In the rush of final development and the commencement of marketing, far too many businesses never get around to checking on the strength of the trademarks chosen for the new product. The real cost of trademark management is not searching and registration fees: The real cost is the tremendous damage to marketing momentum incurred when a new product must hastily be renamed when infringement is discovered, or perhaps a license must be obtained for the unwitting use of another company's trademark. Worse still is when a valuable market is created by the product, competitors then appropriate the company's trademark names or designs, and the company discovers that its mark is defectively weak or otherwise unenforceable against "infringers." The company forfeits the tradefame and marketing lead developed at great expense.

These scenarios can be avoided. The cost is chiefly in management: acknowledging the importance of trademarks and the need for coherent management of trademarks as the valuable asset that they are.

How to Get Some Assurance

First, come up with a striking and nondescriptive name or mark (given the industry you are in). Just as Apple is good, Digital Equipment Corporation is bad; it works only because of the significant fame of the company in and out of its own industry.

Second, check the candidate name against industry directories, product encyclopedias, and telephone books in major cities. Call the Secretaries of State in major states (most all will respond to telephone inquiries as to availability of tradenames and marks). Search online to determine the use of the proposed mark by others. Should distribution in foreign countries be anticipated, take a look in those markets as well. At that point, a professional search is in order, for either the United States or other countries as needed. Legal counsel is required to provide an opinion as to the availability and relative strength of the name or mark.

Guidelines for the Proper Use of Trademarks

With ownership of trademarks comes specific responsibilities, if the right of ownership is to be preserved. The duties revolve around two general issues:

1. Giving customers, suppliers, prospects, and the public notice that the company considers a product name a genuine trademark.
2. Monitoring your industry for the use of marks that may be deceptively similar to the company's mark, and providing the users of such confusing marks clear and specific notice that their mark is infringing, and to terminate its use in that form.

Explicit notice of trademark ownership is necessary both to preserve one's own marks, and to avoid running afoul of the owners of other marks used by the company in its literature and marketing.

The key is *reasonable notice,* which means somewhere in each use of the mark. In a promotional piece or advertisement, notice should be included once in the beginning and/or at the end in written out form. Notices should appear on product labels, packaging, documentation, shipping labels. In regard to service marks, notices should appear on all commercial documents where the mark is used, including reports and invoices.

Furthermore, it is good business practice to acknowledge others' marks referenced in advertisements, documentation, etc. For example, "Panafax™ is a trademark of Panasonic America, Inc." This is critical in regard to references to competitor's marks in your own promotional materials, such as in comparison charts, especially where the marks may be somewhat similar.

A trademark notice must be used once in each piece of printed materials that refers to the trademark. If the trademark notice appears with the first or most prominent use of the trademark in an advertisement or publication, it is not necessary that the notice be repeated each time the trademark is used after that.

Use of the Trademark Symbols ™ and ®

When a trademark has not yet been registered in the Patent and Trademark Office, the letters TM (SM or ™ may be used for service marks) in small capitals can be placed on the "shoulder" of the trademark. Also appropriate is a footnote that says, "Speedbox is a trademark of Digicomp."

The registration symbol (®) is used when the trademark (or servicemark) has been registered in the United States Patent and Trademark Office (PTO). The filing of an application is not the same as getting a registration. It is improper to use ® before the certificate of registration has actually been issued. If deliberate use of a false registration notice is made and the PTO finds out about it, the PTO may refuse to subsequently register the trademark, and the notice may also be unenforceable in court against an infringer.

Any of the following three alternatives can be used for a registered trademark:

❑ Registered in U.S. Patent and Trademark Office

❑ Reg. U.S. Pat. & Tm. Off.

❑ The letter R enclosed within a circle (®)

Trademarks are one of a business's most important assets and should be treated with the care due something so valuable.

Trademark Registrations

Registering a company's trademarks has several important dimensions. First, it establishes a registrant's rights in the mark, including ownership and the right to exclusive use in commerce. Federal registration under the revised federal statute provides that registration constitutes prima facie evidence of the validity of the mark, which, should litigation be required, considerably reduces the burden on the trademark registrant (owner). At least as important, registration establishes a very strong form of notice to would-be users of the same or similar marks. Prudent businesses conduct searches prior to adopting a trademark; registration serves to provide firm notice that a mark is in current use and is apt to be vigorously protected. Federal registration is available for trademarks in use in commerce across state lines, and protects the mark in question throughout the United States, but not in any foreign countries (unlike copyrights). Federal trademark registrations should be handled by an attorney familiar with practice before the Patent and Trademark Office of the U.S. Department of Commerce.

Costs for registration will run from $800 to $2000, depending on the attorney and the difficulty in obtaining a registration. Many attorneys will handle registration on a quoted flat fee basis, provided the application is not contested by an individual or business who files an "opposition" proceeding asserting that the applicant's mark will infringe the opposer's already existing trademark.

For unopposed mark applications, the process takes from ten months to several years. The reason for the lengthy application period and for the associated legal costs is that the federal trademark application process is a contested adversarial proceeding between the applicant and the Trademark Office Examiner assigned to the application. The application and supporting materials are filed, and the Examiner more often than not rejects the application for stated grounds, to which the applicant responds. Time between action cycles is typically three months. So it is easy to see where the time goes.

Once registration has been obtained, the company's comptroller or general counsel should be alerted as to the future necessity for filings with the Trademark Office, and the dates should be reliably entered into the business's perpetual calender.

1. An affidavit of use for the trademark must be filed during the sixth year following registration. If such an affidavit is not filed, the mark registration will be cancelled by the Trademark Office. The purpose of this is to remove "deadwood" from the registration roles. Notice of this requirement is attached to the registration certificate.

2. Renewal for an additional 20-year term must be filed once the initial one of the same period has run.

Purchase or acquisition of registered trademarks, most often in conjunction with purchase or licensing accompanying products or technology, requires that a formal written assignment of the trademark registration be filed with the Trademark Office. While such an assignment can be accomplished later, perhaps when litigation warrants it, obtaining the prompt assistance of the previous owner is sure to be easier at the time of transfer than years later.

Tradenames

The tradename of a business may or may not be the same as its legal name. The legal name may be either the corporation's name as it appears on its Articles of Incorporation filed with the Secretaries of States in the states it does business, or its "doing business as" or "dba" name in the case of partnerships or sole proprietorships. A single business may have many tradenames used in different markets, industries, or product lines.

Whatever the tradename, it must be registered as such in the legal jurisdiction in which it is being used. This requirement originates from the need to identify a legally responsible person or corporation "behind" a business operating under another name.

In most states, tradename registration is with the Secretary of State, while in some registration is on a local level, with the city clerk in the city in which the principal place of business is located. Procedures are straightforward and fees are minimal; typically registration can be handled competently without recourse to counsel.

Registrations must be made in each and every state within which the business has a "business presence" in a technical, legal sense. The nature of this presence is a function of state statute and court-made law, and it varies. At a minimum, the existence of an office for the benefit of the business will establish such a presence. Tradename registrations in foreign jurisdictions may or may not be covered when the business registers with the state or local office that oversees such foreign businesses. This will have to be ascertained on a case-by-case basis, and advice of counsel familiar with the laws of the jurisdiction is suggested.

Enforcement of Rights

Valuable trademark rights must be protected if they are to be preserved. Protection does not stop at the correct use of notices and registrations in the jurisdictions where the trademark is in use. Equally important is a coherent and comprehensive trademark enforcement plan.

The key is knowledge about potentially infringing marks. The company's primary industry and related channels of commerce should be routinely surveyed to monitor for the entry of competitors who may be using identical or similar trademarks. The reason for monitoring related channels of commerce is to protect the company's ability to move into new complementary markets where the existing trademark could be a valuable asset.

For example, the Honda Motor Company did not use new trademarks when it expanded from the manufacture and distribution of motorcycles to automobiles and power equipment such as generators and lawn mowers. Rather, it leveraged its fame as a designer and constructor of innovative and high-quality motorcycles to create an immediate market presence in new channels of commerce, by using its Honda™ trademark on the new types of products.

Trademark monitoring is best approached from two angles. First, someone in-house may be assigned the task to review industry publications to watch for new product and new company announcements, with an eye towards trademarks and tradenames that may be similar if not identical to those of the company. The second angle is to secure the services of an attorney or trademark service firm to review the *Patent & Trademark Office Gazette* for new trademarks that have been approved by the Patent Office. If a problematic mark is discovered in the *Gazette*, an "opposition" proceeding may be commenced by the company in the Patent Office to request that the "new" mark not be registered on the basis of the preexisting rights of the company. Opposition actions will for most businesses be delegated to trademark counsel, in light of the specialized and technical nature of the proceedings before the Patent Office.

Successfully Dealing with the Trademark Infringer

The most typical scenario is for the company to discover on its own (often through industry publications or trade shows) that a new or existing competitor has commenced use of a trademark similar to one of its own. Not uncommonly, current customers will tip you off that there is a "new guy" on the block using a similar trademark. There have also been instances where customers or would-be customers of the new product call your company for orders or product support!

The most appropriate response upon such a discovery is to immediately contact the company suspected of infringement. This should be done in writing, in a letter to the company president that asserts two equally important points:

1. Your company has the right to exclusive use of the trademark in question.
2. The competitor must immediately discontinue its use of the trademark. A specified date should be given, by which time the other company should confirm its agreement or expect formal legal action.

If no response is received in the specified time, a telephone call is in order, with the person with whom ultimate responsibility for the potential business liability lies. Assume it is the president or other chief operating officer, unless you are told otherwise.

Generally, the most productive tactic is a firm but politic posture, that acknowledges the competitor's position and seeks to assist in devising a transition mechanism that will ultimately serve your company's ultimate objective—preservation of the strength of its trademark.

Few instances of trademark infringement are intentional or done in knowledge of the trademark and unfair competition laws. Whether or not the perpetrators *should* know is another question. The important fact is that the business problem of competing and confusing trademarks is more often than not solved most efficiently by skilled and open-minded negotiations that address the needs and objectives of both sides.

At times it is appropriate to seek an immediate injunction against a competitor using a confusing mark to one of your own, but this should not be the default position.

Correction of the trademark use by a competitor that is causing the confusion must be carefully considered. If the mark in question is strong, care must be taken that the company does not abandon its right to the broadest use of the mark. More typically, it is possible to suggest that the competitor merely modify the trademark, perhaps by incorporating the company name into the trademark and design elements. This will often eliminate potential confusion, where the original use and the competitor's use of the mark were not identical, and where the original user may well not have a legally enforceable claim to that form of use of the trademark.

In any event, a negotiated solution should be reduced to a writing signed by both companies. The agreement can simply set out that:

❏ A controversy arose over the status of the use by the parties of the specified trademarks.

❏ In functional language, what the competitor has agreed to in regard to restrictions on marks it may use.

This written agreement is very important, because it is not unheard of for these problems to reappear a few years down the road, with the arrival of new management or marketing staff.

The Business Importance of Copyright Management

Copyrighted materials, like trademarks, are always present in the business environment. Copyright, as a legal tool, is a protection mechanism of great usefulness for many types of business assets.

While the most common form of work protectable by copyright consists of materials such as books, documentation, and other printed media, much more is covered, including computer software, film and video, three-dimensional works, and sound recordings.

What Is a Copyright?

Copyright is not always well understood. Copyright protects only the expressions of those things as can be perceived by sight or sound; copyrights do not protect intellectual ideas, concepts, or underlying conceptual designs.

This book is copyrighted, which is to say that the manner in which the subject matter is organized and developed is protected against most types of unauthorized copying. But anyone is free to use—even "copy"—the ideas and concepts contained here.

A copyright exists from the moment in time that an eligible work is created in fixed form; that is, it is an incident of the process of authorship. No registration or other types of governmental filings are required to "create" a copyright, although, as we will explore, there are substantial benefits in certain situations.

The book that you are reading is protected by copyright, but the ideas are there for you and others to do with what you will. The copyright owner literally owns the exclusive right to copy—to reproduce—the literal page, painting, drawing, song, computer instruction set (expressed either in software or in the form of a computer chip or "firmware"), trademark logo, ad infinitum.

Copyright law is federal law (Title 17 of the United States Code), and so does not vary from state to state. Additionally, the United States is a member of the major international copyright conventions; so securing a valid copyright in the United States generally assures a U.S. business of copyright protection worldwide without additional action. The significant exception to this rule is computer software, which some countries treat in a more restricted fashion than the United States for copyright purposes.

What Is Protectable by Copyright?

Copyright applies to an "original work of authorship" the moment it is fixed in a tangible form of expression. The key words are "originality" and "authorship." Generally almost anything commercially valuable that is potentially copyrightable meets the creative authorship test. Originality is a bit more difficult, and can best be explained by explaining what is not original. Copyright protects authorship that is not based on or derived from something else; hence the protection for *derivative works* based on an already existing copyrighted work. Without getting into an arcane area of judge-made caselaw, it can be said that, if you are concerned that a work is substantially similar to another work, it probably is.

Something need not be directly perceivable by human eyes or ears to be copyrightable; while a legal hurdle in the past, use of a machine or process to perceive or communicate a work does not preclude copyright. Examples are phonograph records, microfiche, and computer software. The copyright laws had to be amended to cover phonograph records during the early years of that industry. More recently, controversy arose over the applicability of copyright to computer software and firmware (code physically manifested within a computer chip). This controversy was eliminated by the Software Copyright Act of 1980, which expressly added software to the categories of copyrightable works. It is important to note, however, that this controversy persists in some foreign countries.

Copyright protection is applicable for almost every area of a business's work product. This includes:

❑ Printed material such as marketing and sales materials, internal handbooks and policy guides, contracts, customer lists and information, product documentation, support and technical information, and information and collections of data regarding production and distribution management and operations.

❑ Still photographs, film and video materials pertaining to products or sales and marketing, internal operations, and employee and customer training and education.

❑ Computer software, developed or purchased for both internal use or commercial distribution.

❑ Graphics and other artwork used for logos, advertising, both in and of itself and as used in conjunction with products.

❑ Maps, globes, charts, technical drawings, diagrams, models, blueprints, and other drawings and designs reduced to a visually or aurally perceivable form.

Copyright protects the expressions of intangibles, not the intangibles themselves; so certain fundamental categories of valuable business assets are inherently unprotectable by copyright:

❑ Ideas, procedures, methods, systems, processes, concepts, principles, discoveries, or devices, as distinguished from a description, explanation, or illustration.

❑ Works consisting entirely of information that is common property and containing no original authorship. For example, standard calendars, generic business forms, height and weight charts, tape measures and rules, and lists or tables taken from public documents or other common sources.

❑ Works that have not been fixed in a tangible form of expression. For example, works that may have been contemporaneously discussed in meetings but never notated or recorded in a memorandum, sketch, or any manner.

❑ Titles, names, short phrases, and slogans; familiar symbols or designs; mere variations of typographic ornamentation, lettering, or coloring; mere listings of ingredients or contents.

Scope of Copyright Protection for Computer Software

The breadth of protection for computer software is an area in flux, and will likely continue to be so for some time, in the United States and abroad. Copyright protection clearly extends to both human-readable source code and machine-readable object code. How far beyond these criteria the copyright extends is the question.

Some structure is clearly protected, including the structure, sequence, and organization of a program, even where no literal code is copied. The key is the ability of the allegedly infringing programmer to have implemented the same concepts and program objectives in a different structure or sequence. Should there be but one way to implement a given objective, there should therefore be no infringement.

The area of "look and feel" is an area of much more uncertainty at present. Under current Copyright Office procedure, a program's user interface in the form of screen displays is subject to copyright protection under the underlying program's copyright registration as a literary work. No additional audiovisual registration is required. The extent of the protection granted is, however, an area of controversy.

Benefits of Copyright

Copyright protection is available to both published and unpublished works (the meaning of "publication" for copyright purposes is discussed in a later section of this chapter). The Copyright Act generally gives the owner of copyright the exclusive right to do and to authorize others to:

❑ Make copies of the copyrighted work.

❑ Prepare "derivative works" (modifications or developments) based on the copyrighted work.

❑ Distribute copies of the copyrighted work to the public by sale or other transfer of ownership, or by rental, lease, or lending.

❑ Perform or display the copyrighted work publicly, in the case of literary, film, video, soundtrack, graphic, pictorial works.

It is illegal for anyone to violate any of the rights provided to the owner of copyright. These rights, however, are not unlimited in scope, and in some cases, these limitations are specified exemptions from copyright liability. One major limitation is the doctrine of *fair use*, and in other instances the limitation takes the form of a *compulsory license*, under which certain limited uses of copyrighted works are permitted upon payment of specified royalties and compliance with statutory conditions.

Establishing Copyright Ownership

The copyright owner can literally be anyone, and must be made a matter of clear agreement if more than one party is involved. Who wrote the work? Was it a consultant who may not have explicitly agreed that the work was a work for hire? Was it an employee who arguably may not have been acting within his or her formal job description? This is a big area for problems, if there is an absence of agreement. And the agreement should be in writing.

If a copyrighted work was created by a company principal, there may still exist troubling uncertainty as to ownership. This is particularly problematic if the creation was wholly or partially completed prior to the founding of the company. It may be that the principal intended that the company was only to have contingent rights in the copyrighted work while he or she was involved in the company, or intended to assign copyright interests to the company for only a fixed term or until the company is sold, etc. These types of issues must be addressed at the earliest possible time. More and more investors are becoming sensitive to issues of ownership status of KI assets, including copyrighted property, and due diligence is rapidly starting to include the ownership status of KI assets critical to the value and future success of businesses in which they are placing investments.

In any event, there should be written documentation or an agreement to support the argument that a certain person is the copyright owner, if the alleged copyright owner is an individual or business other than the human being that actually wrote the work.

Upon creation of copyrighted work, the copyright in the work of authorship immediately becomes the property of the author who created it. Only the author or those deriving their rights through the author can rightfully claim copyright.

Copyrighted works arising from within an employment relationship are covered by the *work for hire doctrine* of copyright law. In the case of works made for hire, the employer and not the employee is presumptively considered the author. There are often problems surrounding this issue, however, and extensive and ongoing recent litigation emphasizes the reality of it.

Businesses must acknowledge that ownership of copyright can and will often be challenged by authors when the fact of that ownership becomes valuable. Relationships with outside consultants must clearly specify in writing that the work commissioned is a work for hire, and that, if for any reason the work is declared not a work for hire, that the author transfers and assigns all interests in copyright and other ownership interests to the contracting company. Simple forethought and incorporation of this mechanism into standard company policy will eliminate this uncertainty.

Employment agreements must address this issue as well: All copyrighted work performed during the period of employment is a work for hire. Again, if for any reason the work is declared not a work for hire, the author or employee transfers and assigns all interests in copyright and other ownership interests to the employer.

The authors of a joint work are co-owners of the copyright in the work, unless there is an expressed agreement to the contrary.

Copyright in each separate contribution to a periodical or other collective work is distinct from copyright in the collective work as a whole and vests initially with the author of the contribution included within the compilation.

Mere "ownership" of a copyrighted work does not give the possessor the copyright. The law provides that a transfer of ownership of any material object that embodies a protected work does not of itself convey any rights in the copyright. This is critically important to remember. Purchase of rights in a copyrighted work must expressly transfer the copyright if it is in fact to be validly conveyed.

How to Create and Maintain Copyright Notices

When a work is published under the authority of the copyright owner, it is useful to place a notice of copyright on all publicly distributed copies. Notice is no longer required by law, but is important in educating the public that the copyrighted work is considered proprietary, copyrighted material by the owner. Additionally, it creates a presumption of knowledge by a copier who had access that the work is copyrighted, should enforcement of copyright be required. Accurate and correct copyright notices should be an integral part of every business's KI asset strategy.

The preferred form for copyright notices is:

© [year] [copyright owner]. All Rights Reserved.

© is the internationally recognized symbol for copyright. It should be used wherever possible. Where it is not possible (computer font limitations, for example), use "copyright" or "copr." in preference to "(c)." For educational purposes, the full word "copyright" may certainly be used along with ©.

The year in the notice is the date that the work was first published, that is, commercially distributed (discussed in detail later in the chapter). As already discussed, the copyright applies to the original work of authorship plus derivative works based on that original work (revisions, enhancements, software bug fixes). So the year for notice purposes stays the same for the entire life of distribution unless the work itself changes substantively. When the work *is* substantively changed (new topics added, significant editing done, etc.), cumulative dates be used.

Computer software is typically rereleased on a regular basis with substantive changes. Genuinely new code and logic structures that perform the same final functions as previous code and new code and logic structures that effect new functions should be considered new works of authorship and copyrighted separately. This means one new date if the new work completely replaces the previous work, or more likely a cumulative notice. A full rewrite can use the single year of publication of the new version.

In the case of complications or derivative works incorporating previously published material, the year date of first publication of the compilation or derivative work is sufficient. The year date may be omitted completely for pictorial, graphic, or sculptural works, or any useful articles. The name in the notice must be the name of the owner of copyright in the work, an abbreviation by which the name can be recognized, or a generally known alternative designation of the owner. The term "All Rights Reserved" is legally required in copyright notices in certain South American countries. It is a matter of good practice simply to incorporate it in all copyright notices.

Position of Notice

The notice should be affixed to copies of the work in such a manner and location as to "give reasonable notice of the claim of copyright." The position is not critical, but generally should be placed in the first pages of printed material, and on labels for packaged media such as audio, video, or computer tapes, and computer diskettes. For computer software, it is important to include a notice in source and object code, as applicable, within the user interface for application software.

Licensing and Acquisition Issues Regarding Copyrighted Property

A business's copyrighted property is the subject of various types of transfers: limited licensing, sale (with or without copyright), lease, and loan. Inversely, companies will be acquiring new KI assets, which themselves are copyrighted.

Any or all of the exclusive rights, or any subdivision of those rights, of the copyright owner may be transferred, but the transfer of exclusive rights is not valid unless that transfer is in writing and signed by the owner of the rights conveyed (or such owner's duly authorized agent). Transfer of a right on a nonexclusive basis does not require a writing.

This means that businesses seeking to acquire full ownership of copyrighted materials must be critically aware of the necessity of properly structured agreements for the transfer. The key is expressed, unambiguous transfer of the copyright in the book, software, or other copyrighted material, in addition to rights of exclusive possession, duplication, distribution, modification, etc., which may also be the subject of the transfer.

A copyright may also be conveyed by operation of law and may be bequeathed by will or pass as personal property by the applicable laws of intestate succession, when the owner of the copyright dies without a will.

Copyright is a personal property right, and it is subject to the various state laws and regulations that govern the ownership, inheritance, or transfer of personal property as well as terms of contracts or conduct of business.

Recordation of transfers of copyright ownership may be made in the Copyright Office. Although recordation is not required to make a valid transfer as between the parties, it provides certain legal advantages and in certain instances may be required to validate the transfer against claims by third parties.

When and How to Secure Federal Copyright Registration

In general, copyright registration is a legal formality intended to make a public record of the basic facts of a particular copyright. However, registration is not a condition of copyright protection. Even though registration is not generally a requirement for protection, the copyright law provides several inducements or advantages to encourage copyright owners to make registration. Among these advantages are the following:

❏ Registration establishes a public record of the copyright claim.

❏ Registration is ordinarily necessary before any infringement suits may be filed in court.

❏ If made before or within five years of publication, registration will establish prima facie evidence in court of the validity of the copyright and of the facts stated in the certificate.

❏ If registration is made within three months after publication of the work or prior to an infringement of the work, statutory damages and attorney's fees will be available to the copyright owner in court actions. Otherwise, only an award of actual damages and profits is available to the copyright owner.

Registration may be made at any time within the life of the copyright. Unlike the law before 1978, when a work has been registered in unpublished form, it is not necessary to make another registration when the work becomes published (although the copyright owner may register the published edition, if desired).

A work does not need to be registered with the United States Copyright Office in order for it to be protectable. Indeed, the fact that a work was not registered at the time of its infringement in no way dilutes its protectability. Registration is, however, a procedural prerequisite to bringing a copyright infringement suit.

Correspondence concerning registration and the required deposit copies may be addressed to the Register of Copyrights, Copyright Office, Washington, D.C. 20559.

7
Security Issues

The Internet is still new marketing territory. Early commercial failures can be attributed to lack of patience and perhaps lack of preparation. Commercially successful ventures have found a way to promote themselves within the etiquette of the net with products that, by design or accident, appeal to the subculture of the web. Growth in the number of accesses has been exciting to chart. Combined, our stores are seeing between four and five thousand hits per day after starting out at around one hundred per day eight months ago. Sales will explode as customers gain more confidence in the security of putting their money, whether in the form of credit card, electronic check, or digital cash, on the cyber salescounter.

Larry Cullimore
Cybershop Proprietor
Due North Multimedia
http://www.icw.com/duenorth/duenorth.html
Net Sweats & Tees
http://www.icw.com/netsweat/netsweat.html

"Gone to Hell in a Handbasket!"

If you're looking for an easy way to lose money, destroy customer confidence, waste your investment capital and labor, invite law suits, put your employees out of work, and just about guarantee the destruction of your business, then all you have to do is fail to protect certain information that you and your Internet customers will want to exchange.

Naturally, you would never intentionally set out to achieve such goals. However, that's exactly what can happen if you fail to take a few precautionary steps before setting up shop online! As the person legally, financially, and otherwise responsible for the conduct of your business, you have a responsibility to provide for a secure environment in which such information can be exchanged without risk to either party.

As you read this book, thousands of storefront owners and customers are exchanging information in the course of conducting business. Much of this information, while not intended for viewing by the general public, is benign and, even if made public, could serve no illegal purpose. For example, somewhere out there on the Internet, a customer and storefront owner are exchanging information regarding the latest New Age music from Kitaro. But who really cares if Barry What's His Name from Bend, Indiana is wild about Kitaro's latest CD?

Other information being exchanged on the Net is sensitive, confidential, valuable, and privileged. It is intended to be viewed only by the sender and receiver. Unfortunately, and often tragically, and without the knowledge of either party, certain information is being intercepted by prying eyes whose intent is to spy on other people or, worse, to use the unauthorized information in an illegal or malicious manner. With the right kind of knowledge, anyone can gain access to any unprotected information that is being transmitted via the Internet. And as difficult as it may seem, information about how to accomplish such a feat is available from the Internet itself.

Simply put, any information that is being transmitted from one computer to another, if unprotected, is accessible to prying eyes.

Can you imagine the damage if the following information, as collected by you for use in running your business, found its way to the general public?

- ❏ Customer credit card numbers
- ❏ Confidential business proposals
- ❏ Personal letters
- ❏ Internal sales reports

❏ Prelaunch product designs and specifications reports

❏ Employee evaluation and performance records

❏ Price quotes

❏ Call for bids

❏ Home mailing address

❏ Personal phone numbers

❏ Bank and checking account numbers

❏ Directory of corporate charitable sponsors

❏ Employee records

Watch What You Say!

In any computer network, whether it be a local network within a single company and closed to the general public, or one as large and as open as the Internet, information that is sent from one computer to another can be viewed, if unprotected, by anyone trained in such matters who has access to the network.

A favorite pasttime of hackers (talented computer programmers who intentionally try to gain access to restricted data and information on remote computer network systems) is to intercept e-mail messages or files being transmitted by unsuspecting Internet users.

The golden rule, therefore, when you become an Internet traveler is to consider all information that you send or receive to be *public access information*—information that may become known to anyone, anywhere, at any time. So, unless your information is protected from prying eyes, watch what you say online. Never include any information in any transmission of any kind that, if it became publicly known, would bring harm to you or another person.

How, Then, Can Information Be Protected?

Several leading companies have developed a means of converting or coding computer information that, when viewed by someone who does not have a conversion program, becomes unintelligible. This process of coding information is referred to as *data encryption*. Actually, the use of data encryption can be traced back hundreds of years as an accepted method of protecting information from the wrong eyes.

For example, a regular, uncoded e-mail message may look like this:

Dear Bob,

Thanks for the background information about your new boss, Bill. Yes, I agree, he's one major jerk and should be fired. Let's hope he's gone soon, so we can get back to our normal routine of doing nothing around here.

Fred

Certainly, this is not the kind of information that you would want to place in the public domain. However, after encryption, the same information might look like this if it was intercepted by the wrong party:

464927647586898RUHF7YFG7356TR5JT9KJY8F67E56T34TR564
HRT758U5757657T675Y39FKTY905-=2=R059R7872UR9
28REHGF820-DF.H;J',/,'K][R9028UYE

RSA Data Security, Inc. of Redwood City, California is a company that has developed the industry's leading encryption technology, a program referred to as RSA Public Key Cryptosystem. Telecommunication devices, such as phones, faxes, and computers that are equipped with this technology can now be used to securely transmit information via standard phone lines and the Internet.

This technology is so good at encrypting information (no one has been able to crack the code yet), that it has been adopted for use by some of the nation's leading companies, such as Netscape, Visa, MCI, Microsoft, Lotus, CompuServe, and many others. RSA technology is so foolproof that even the federal government is concerned about its use, since it can't intercept communications on the Internet that it deems illegal or in violation of some federal law, as it can be placing a wire tap on a phone conversation.

How Does Encryption Work?

The RSA technology operates on the principle of a two-key (coded) system. One key (code) is used for encrypting information while the other key (code) is for decryption. No two key combinations are the same, and both keys assigned to you must be used together to actually encrypt or decrypt information. To use the system you keep one key private, not telling anyone its code, while the other key is public and you may share it with anyone you wish.

If you wish to encrypt a document, you would first key it with the recipient's known public code. Therefore, since the document can now only be decrypted by the recipient's private key, you know no other person can read the document and can now be sent safely via any electronic means.

This system works like a voice mail system. With such a system, you are assigned both a phone number (including a mailbox number) and a password. The phone number/mailbox combination is public and may be given out to anyone you wish. People may then call in and leave you messages in your mailbox. However, since only you know your password, only you can gain access to your messages. The public phone number/mailbox and your private password provide you with a secure means of communication.

In addition to providing a high level of secure data transfer, the use of encryption technology offers another benefit. When encrypted, a transmission, such as a document, can contain a "digital signature" of the sender, a unique code that only the sender can attach to the data about to be transmitted. By incorporating digital signatures, the receiver can be assured of the identify of the person transmitting the document, as well as the authenticity of the document itself. The security of this digital signature process is so good that it is considered by courts of law to be the equivalent of a person's signature.

How Can a Storefront Owner Incorporate Encryption Technology?

As stated earlier in this book, a Web browser is a special software program used to access storefronts on the Internet, by both the storefront owner and by customers. By using a Web browser equipped with encryption technology, and by requiring your customers to do the same, both parties can then transfer information back and forth that cannot be read by a third party.

When both parties are using a Web browser equipped with encryption technology, such sensitive information as credit card numbers can easily and securely be transmitted.

What If My Customer Is Not Using Encryption Technology?

When your customers are about to transmit sensitive information (such as when they are about to enter and send credit card numbers to make a purchase), the server (computer) housing your storefront can be instructed to examine the customers' browsers. If they are found not to have encryption technology, the following notice can be displayed on screen:

Warning!

Your Web browser does not contain encryption technology. Therefore, the secure transmission of sensitive data, such as your credit card number, cannot be guaranteed.

Do you wish to:

Proceed

If you select this option, you assume the complete responsibility for the transmission of your data. While we will make every effort to ensure it is not misused, we cannot guarantee such assurance.

Download New Browser

You are invited to download a copy of a new browser (free of charge) that contains encryption technology. By installing it on your computer, and then by using it to revisit our storefront, you may transmit information securely and with complete confidence.

Cancel

Stop this transaction.

Naturally, most sensible individuals will download the free browser and return to your storefront to purchase.

Several Web browsers can be obtained free of charge, and copies distributed without cost to you and your customers, from various services on the Internet. To obtain a Web browser with encryption technology, contact one of the following companies:

Company/service	URL address
CommerceNet	http://www.commerce.net
I-Link	http://i-linkcom.com
MCI	http://www.internetmci.com
Netscape	http://www.netscape.com

See App. C, "Internet Resource Directory," for additional resources. Several Web browsers with encryption technology can be downloaded free of charge from several locations on the Internet. Note the URL preceding address for those options.

Web browsers are interchangeable, regardless of the Internet access service provider that you selected. You may, if you prefer, replace the Web browser supplied to you by your access service with one that contains encryption technology.

If you do not plan to request sensitive information from your customers, and if you do not plan to transfer sensitive information to other people via the Internet, then you need not use a Web browser equipped with encryption technology.

At the time of the writing of this book, NetCruiser did not contain encryption technology. However, you should contact NetCom to inquire if a new update is available that does contain encryption technology. If so, it is more than likely that you can download a copy from NetCom using your existing NetCruiser software program.

8
Actual Storefronts in Use Today

> We put up a home page on our retail location in Houston as a market test in September of 1994 that included a catalog request form that could be returned to us via e-mail. We averaged over five requests and 65 "people in the store" a day. The activity was mostly weekdays, and consisted of mostly educators, students, or professionals, which is exactly our demographics.
>
> We put up the Windsurf Webhouse in February 1995 as a stand-alone store and subsequently sold two boards, two carbon fiber booms, and various other parts.
>
> We feel we are in early in the grand scheme of things, but we were the first with a wind surfing store on the Web. We are extremely excited with our results to date.
>
> **Charles Giorelli**
> President of Windsurfing Sports, Inc.
> 1-800-WHY SAIL
> http://www.sccsi.com/windsurf/webhouse.html

If there were a master list of all storefronts in use today (which is not likely), it would be much longer than the list found in this chapter, and would occupy far more space than available here! The list found in this chapter represents only a sampling of the thousands of storefronts already in operation on the Internet. Some are serious business ventures, others are more bent on public relations or the sharing of information, while a select few are humorous in nature and serve only to bring a smile to our faces as we travel through cyberspace. Nonetheless, they all illustrate the range of possibilities: The Internet is truly open to all those who wish to participate.

You are encouraged to visit each storefront, viewing for yourself the diversity of creativity that exists, how other folks have set up shop, and how business is conducted electronically on the Net.

Use the NetCruiser software program and its Web browser function to visit each site. Just enter the URL address and, as they say, you'll be surfing the Net. The storefronts that the authors found particularly interesting are listed in **bold print** for easy identification. Remember: URL addresses are case-sensitive; so enter the address exactly as listed, with upper and lower case letters as indicated. If you get an error message or any other message after attempting to visit a site, you may have entered the address incorrectly, or the site is down for repairs or closed.

See App. C, "Internet Resource Directory," for a listing of books that contain other lists of Web storefronts and sites.

Remember! The Internet is in constant change. Certain Web sites listed may no longer be in existence today, or may have different URL addresses. If you can't connect, try using Yahoo to determine if the site is still on the Net.

The best of the Web includes ...

Gastrointestinal and Liver Pathology
http://www.pds.med.umich.edu/users/greenson/

HomeStyles Home Plans
http://homestyles.com/hs/

McMaster University
http://www.mcmaster.ca/

The Miramara
http://www.seanet.com/Users/deanl/miramar.html

The Nordic Pages
http://www.algonet.se/~nikos/nordic.html

Old Towne Canoe Company
http://www.cybermalls.com/cywharf/oldtown/index.html

The Improbable Players: Drama for Alcohol and Drug Abuse Prevention
http://www.xwnsei.com/users/players

Web Street Mall
http://www.webstreetmall.com/mall

OTA's Native American Resource Page
http://www.ota.gov/nativea.html

Entrepreneurs on the Web
http://sashimi.wwa.com/~notime/eotw/EOTW.htm

African Connexion
http://www.northcoast.com/unlimited/product_directory/african_
connexion/african_connexion.html

Made in America!
http://www.icw.com/america/made.html

Welcome to the White House
http://www.whitehouse.gov/

McDonnell Douglas Aerospace (NASA)
http://www.pat.mdc.com/

Smithsonian Institution
http://www.si.edu/

Our Daily Bread
http://unicks.calvin.edu/daily-bread/

The Trojan Room Coffee Machine
http://www.cl.cam.ac.uk/cgi-bin/xvcoffee

LeLouvre Museum
http://www.cnam.fr/louvre/

Internet Career Connection
http://iccweb.com

Parsons Technology
http://www.shopping2000.com/shopping2000/parsons/

Apartments on Video
http://www.cts.com:80/~aptonvid/

Pete's Fishing Guide Service & Lodging
http://alaskan.com/vendors/pete's.html

Evergreen Internet
http://cybemart.com/

Sundance Resort and Conference Center
http://cybermart.com/sundance/resort/accom.html

San Diego Opera
http://www.infopost.com/cgi-bin/imagemap/client?103,109

Morgantown High School Homepage
http://www.mountain.net/Pinnacle/mhswww/mhshome.html

Scottso the Clown
http://mmink.cts.com/mmink/dossiers/scottso.html

Go! Disks
http://www.demon.co.uk/godisks/index.html

The On-Line Allergy Center
http://www.sig.net/

Solvang, California
http://www.geninc.com/geni/USA/CA/Solvang/travel/

The Stork Delivers
http://www.rai.com/

9

Internet Access Service Providers and Storefront Developers

This chapter contains a listing of resources that you will need when developing an electronic storefront.

Internet Access Service Providers

These companies provide, for a fee, access to the Internet. By connecting your computer to their computer, via your modem and phone line, you can obtain indirect access to the Internet. As stated earlier in this book, use of an indirect access to the Internet is recommended over the more costly option of setting up your own direct Internet location. If you elect to follow this recommendation, you will need the services of an access provider.

Some companies provide limited access, such as e-mail only, while others provide full access, including e-mail, File Transfer Protocol (FTP), Gopher, Internet Relay Chat (IRC), Mailing Lists and Usenet News, Telnet, and World Wide Web. In addition, some companies also provide storefront development services (i.e., programming and database management expertise) to individuals who wish to set up a storefront on the Internet. Check the profile of each service to determine which services are available. Whenever possible, try to select an access service closest to your home or office location to avoid or reduce long-distance phone charges.

It is possible to find an Internet access service provider who is also a storefront developer and, from one service, obtain all the necessary assistance you need to gain access to the Internet and to create your own storefront.

For each listing, the following information is presented:

Service: (company name)
Access: (area serviced by the service provider)
Contact: (name)
E-mail: (address)
Phone: (number)
Fax: (number)

The data used to produce this list was drawn from the InterNIC Leased Line Providers list published via the Internet by InterNIC, a project of the National Science Foundation, and is reprinted here with permission.

Note: Access to the Internet is also available from all of the major commercial computer network services. For additional information, contact the services directly:

America Online
8619 Westwood Center Drive
Vienna, VA 22182
800-827-6364

CompuServe
5000 Arlington Centre Boulevard
Columbus, OH 43220
800-848-8199

Delphi
1030 Massachusetts Avenue
Cambridge, MA 02138
800-695-4005

GEnie
401 N. Washington Street
Rockville, MD 20580
800-638-9636

PRODIGY
445 Hamilton Avenue
White Plains, NY 10601
800-284-5933

Storefront Developers

These companies provide programming and database management services to individuals who wish to develop an electronic storefront. Some of these companies specialize exclusively in storefront development, requiring you to find your own Internet access service provider. Some companies may also provide Internet access service.

For each listing, the following information may be available:

Developer: (person or company name)
Contact: (name)
URL: (address)
Street: (address)
City, State, Zip
Phone: (number)
Fax: (number)
E-mail: (address)

Note: For some listings, not all of this information is available; often only a person's name or company name and URL address are listed. This usually indicates that the persons or companies listed wish to be contacted via their URL address. When no traditional mailing address, phone or fax number, or e-mail address is provided, the reader is directed to contact the source via the URL address. This can be easily accomplished using the NetCruiser Web browser function. Once you reach the Web location, searching the various storefronts or malls often reveals a contact name and additional methods of contact.

Internet Access Service Providers

Service: AlterNet
A service of UUNET Technologies, Inc.
Access: Nationwide
E-mail: alternet-info@uunet.uu.net
Phone: (800) 4UUNET3

Service: ACM Network Services
Access: Nationwide
Contact: Angela Abbott
E-mail: account-info@acm.org
Phone: (817) 776-6876
Fax: (817) 751-7785

Service: American Information Systems
Access: Illinois
Contact: Josh Schneider
E-mail: schneid@ais.net
Phone: (708) 413-8400
Fax: (708) 413-8401

Service: ANS
Access: Nationwide
Contact: Sales and Information
E-mail: info@ans.net
Phone: (800) 456-8267
Fax: (703) 758-7717

Service: APK Public Access
Access: Ohio
Contact: Zbigniew Tyrlik
E-mail: support@wariat.org
Phone: (216) 481-9428

Service: BARRNet
Access: California, Nevada
Contact: Sales
E-mail: info@barrnet.net
Phone: (415) 725-1790
Fax: (415) 725-3119

Service: Beckemeyer Development
Access: California
Contact: Sales
E-mail: info@bdt.com
Phone: (510) 530-9637
Fax: (510) 530-0451

Service: California Online!
Access: California
Contact: Christopher Ward
E-mail: cward@calon.com
Phone: (707) 586-3060
Fax: (707) 588-8642

Service: CCnet Communications
Access: California
Contact: Information
E-mail: info@ccnet.com
Phone: (510) 988-0680
Fax: (510) 998-0689

Service: Centurion Technology, Inc.
Access: Florida
Contact: Jeffery Jablow
E-mail: jablow@cent.com
Phone: (813) 572-5556
Fax: (813) 572-1452

Service: CERFnet
Access: Western United States
Contact: CERFnet Hotline
E-mail: sales@cerf.net
Phone: (800) 876-2373, (619) 455-3900
Fax: (619) 455-3990

Service: CICnet
Access: Midwestern United States
Contact: Marketing and Sales Dept.
E-mail: info@cic.net
Phone: (800) 947-4754, (313) 998-6703
Fax: (313) 998-6105

Service: Clark Internet Services
Access: Northeastern United States
Contact: ClarkNet Office
E-mail: info@clark.net
Phone: (800) 735-2258, (410) 730-9764
Fax: (410) 730-9765

Service: Cloud 9 Internet
Access: New York
Contact: Scott Drassinower
E-mail: scottd@cloud9.net
Phone: (914) 682-0626
Fax: (914) 682-0506

Service: CO Supernet
Access: Colorado
Contact: Guy Cook
E-mail: gcook@csn.org
Phone: (303) 296-8202
Fax: (303) 273-3475

Service: CONCERT
Access: North Carolina
Contact: Naomi Courter
E-mail: info@concert.net
Phone: (919) 248-1999
Fax: (919) 248-1405

Service: Connix
Access: Connecticut
Contact: Jim Hogue
E-mail: office@connix.com
Phone: (203) 349-7059

Service: CRL Network Services
Access: California
Contact: Sales
E-mail: sales@crl.com
Phone: (415) 837-5300

Service: CSUnet
Access: California
Contact: Gary Jones
E-mail: nethelp@csu.net
Phone: (310) 985-9661

Service: CTS Network Services
Access: California
Contact: Sales
E-mail: support@cts.com
Phone: (619) 637-3637
Fax: (619) 637-3630

Service: CyberGate, Inc.
Access: Florida
Contact: Dan Sullivan
E-mail: sales@gate.net
Phone: (305) 428-4283
Fax: (305) 428-7977

Service: DFW Internet Services, Inc.
Access: Texas
Contact: Jack Beech
E-mail: sales@dfw.net
Phone: (817) 332-5116
Fax: (817) 870-1501

Service: DHM Information Management
Access: California
Contact: Dirk Harms-Merbitz
E-mail: dharms@dhm.com
Phone: (310) 214-3349
Fax: (310) 214-3090

Service: Digital Express Group, Inc.
Access: Nationwide
Contact: John Todd
E-mail: sales@access.digex.net
Phone: (800) 969-9090
Fax: (301) 220-0477

Service: EarthLink Network, Inc.
Access: California
Contact: Sky Dayton
E-mail: info@earthlink.net
Phone: (213) 644-9500
Fax: (213) 644-9510

Service: The Eden Matrix
Access: Texas
Contact: John Herzer
E-mail: jch@eden.com
Phone: (512) 478-9900
Fax: (512) 478-9936

Service: The Edge
Access: Tennessee
Contact: Tim Choate
E-mail: info@edge.net
Phone: (615) 455-9915
Fax: (615) 454-2042

Service: Escape (Kazan Corp.)
Access: New York
Contact: Sales
E-mail: info@escape.com
Phone: (212) 888-8780
Fax: (212) 832-0344

Service: Evergreen Internet
Access: Arizona
Contact: Phil Broadbent
E-mail: sales@libre.com (FAX)
Phone: (602) 230-9330
Fax: (602) 230-9773

Service: Florida Online
Access: Florida
Contact: Jerry Russell
E-mail: jerry@ditigal.net
Phone: (407) 635-8888
Fax: (407) 635-9050

Service: FullFeed Communications
Access: Wisconsin
Contact: Katie Stachoviak
E-mail: info@fullfeed.com
Phone: (608) 246-4239

Service: FXnet
Access: North and South Carolina
Contact: Sales
E-mail: info@fx.net
Phone: (704) 338-4670
Fax: (704) 338-4679

Service: HoloNet
Access: Nationwide
Contact: HoloNet Staff
E-mail: support@holonet.net
Phone: (510) 704-0160
Fax: (510) 704-8019

Service: Global Enterprise Services
Access: Nationwide
Contact: Sergio Heker, President
E-mail: market@jvnc.net
Phone: (800) 35-TIGER
Fax: (609) 897-7310

Service: IACNet
Access: Ohio
Contact: Devon Sean McCullough
E-mail: info@iac.net
Phone: (513) 887-8877

Service: ICNet
Access: Michigan, Ohio
Contact: Ivars Upatnieks
E-mail: info@ic.net
Phone: (313) 998-0090

Service: IDS World Network
Access: Northeastern United States
Contact: Information
E-mail: info@ids.net
Phone: (800) IDS-1680

Service: Innovative Data Services
Access: Michigan
Contact: Sales
E-mail: info@id.net
Phone: (810) 478-3554
Fax: (810) 478-2950

Service: INS Info Services
Access: Iowa
Contact: Customer Service
E-mail: service@ins.infonet.net
Phone: (800) 546-6587
Fax: (515) 830-0345

Service: INTAC Access Corporation
Access: New Jersey
Contact: Sales
E-mail: info@intac.com
Phone: (201) 944-1417
Fax: (201) 944-1434

Service: InterAccess
Access: Illinois
Contact: Lev Kaye
E-mail: info@interaccess.com
Phone: (800) 967-1580
Fax: (708) 498-3289

Service: The Internet Access Company
Access: Massachusetts
Contact: Sales
E-mail: info@tiac.net
Phone: (617) 276-7200
Fax: (617) 275-2224

Service: Internet Access Online
Access: Ohio
Contact: Sales
E-mail: sales@iac.com
Phone: (514) 887-8877

Service: Internet Atlanta
Access: Georgia
Contact: Dorn Hetzel
E-mail: info@atlanta.com
Phone: (404) 410-9000
Fax: (404) 410-9005

Service: Internet Express
Access: Colorado
Contact: Customer Service
E-mail: service@usa.net

Phone: (800) 592-1240
Fax: (719) 592-1201

Service: Internet On-Ramp, Inc.
Access: Washington
Contact: Sales
E-mail: info@on-ramp.ior.com
Phone: (509) 927-7267
Fax: (509) 927-0273

Service: Internetworks
Access: Nationwide
Contact: Internetworks, Inc.
E-mail: info@i.net
Phone: (503) 233-4774
Fax: (503) 233-4773

Service: Interport Communications Corp.
Access: New York
Contact: Sales and Information
E-mail: info@interport.net
Phone: (212) 989-1128

Service: IQuest Network Services
Access: Indiana
Contact: Robert Hoquim
E-mail: info@iquest.net
Phone: (800) 844-UNIX, (317) 259-5050
Fax: (317) 259-7289

Service: Kaiwan Corp.
Access: California
Contact: Rachel Hwang
E-mail: sales@kaiwan.com
Phone: (714) 638-2139
Fax: (714) 638-0455

Service: Li Net, Inc.
Access: New York
Contact: Michael Reilly
E-mail: questions@li.net
Phone: (516) 476-1168

Service: Lightside, Inc.
Access: California
Contact: Fred Condo
E-mail: lightside@lightside.com

Phone: (818) 858-9261
Fax: (818) 858-8982

Service: Los Nettos
Access: Los Angeles
Contact: Joe Kemp
E-mail: los-nettos-info@isi.edu
Phone: (310) 822-1511
Fax: (310) 823-6714

Service: maine.net, Inc.
Access: Maine
Contact: Andy Robinson
E-mail: atr@maine.net
Phone: (207) 780-6381
Fax: (207) 780-6301

Service: MCSNet
Access: Illinois
Contact: Karl Denninger
E-mail: info@mcs.net
Phone: (312) 248-8649
Fax: (312) 248-8649

Service: MichNet/Merit
Access: Michigan
Contact: Recruiting Staff
E-mail: info@merit.edu
Phone: (313) 764-9430
Fax: (313) 747-3185

Service: MIDnet
Access: Midwestern United States
Contact: Network Inf Ctr
E-mail: nic@westie.mid.net
Phone: (402) 472-7600
Fax: (402) 472-5640

Service: MRNet
Access: Minnesota
Contact: Dennis Fazio
E-mail: info@MR.Net
Phone: (612) 342-2570
Fax: (612) 342-2873

Service: MV Communications
Access: New Hampshire

Contact: Sales
E-mail: info@mv.mv.com
Phone: (603) 429-2223

Service: NEARNET
Access: Northeastern United States
Contact: NEARNET Information Hotline
E-mail: nearnet-join@near.net
Phone: (617) 873-8730
Fax: (617) 873-5620

Service: NeoSoft, Inc.
Access: Texas
Contact: Jay Williams
E-mail: jmw3@neosoft.com
Phone: (713) 684-5969
Fax: (713) 684-5922

Service: NET99
Access: Nationwide
Contact: Joseph Stroup
E-mail: joe@ns.net99.net
Phone: (800) 638-9947
Fax: (602) 249-1161

Service: NetAxis
Access: Connecticut
Contact: Luis Hernandez
E-mail: luis@netaxis.com
Phone: (203) 969-0618
Fax: (203) 921-1544

Service: NETCOM
Access: United States
Contact: Business or Personal Sales
E-mail: info@netcom.com
Phone: (800) 501-8649, (408) 554-8649
Fax: (408) 241-9145

Service: netILLINOIS
Access: Illinois
Contact: Peter Roll
E-mail: proll@illinois.net
Phone: (708) 866-1825
Fax: (708) 866-1857

Service: Network Intensive
Access: California
Contact: Sales and Information
E-mail: info@ni.net
Phone: (800) 273-5600
Fax: (714) 450-8410

Service: The Network Link, Inc.
Access: California
Contact: Steve Froeschke
E-mail: stevef@tnl1.tnwl.com
Phone: (619) 278-5943

Service: NevadaNet
Access: Nevada
Contact: Braddlee
E-mail: braddlee@nevada.edu
Phone: (702) 784-4827
Fax: (702) 784-1108

Service: New Mexico Technet, Inc.
Access: New Mexico
Contact: Marianne Granoff
E-mail: granoff@technet.nm.org
Phone: (505) 345-6555
Fax: (505) 435-6559

Service: New York Net
Access: New York
Contact: Bob Tinkelman
E-mail: sales@new-york.net
Phone: (718) 776-6811
Fax: (718) 217-9407

Service: Northcoast Internet
Access: California
Contact: Kevin Savetz
E-mail: support@northcoast.com
Phone: (707) 443-8696

Service: NorthWest CommLink
Access: Washington
Contact: Garlend Tyacke
E-mail: gtyacke@nwcl.net
Phone: (206) 336-0103

Service: Northwest Nexus, Inc.
Access: Washington
Contact: Information
E-mail: info@nwnexus.wa.com
Phone: (206) 455-3505
Fax: (206) 455-4672

Service: NorthwestNet
Access: Northwestern United States
Contact: Member Relations
E-mail: info@nwnet.net
Phone: (206) 562-3000
Fax: (206) 562-4822

Service: NYSERNet
Access: New York
Contact: Sales
E-mail: info@nysernet.org
Phone: (315) 453-2912
Fax: (315) 453-3052

Service: OARnet
Access: Ohio
Contact: Alison Brown
E-mail: alison@oar.net
Phone: (614) 292-8100
Fax: (614) 292-7168

Service: Old Colorado City Comm
Access: Colorado
Contact: Sales
E-mail: thefox@oldcolo.com
Phone: (719) 528-5849
Fax: (719) 528-5869

Service: PACCOM
Access: Hawaii
Contact: Torben Nielsen
E-mail: torben@hawaii.edu
Phone: (808) 956-3499

Service: PanixEastern
Access: United States
Contact: New User Staff
E-mail: info-person@panix.com
Phone: (212) 741-4400
Fax: (212) 741-5311

Service: Ping
Access: Georgia
Contact: Brett Koller
E-mail: bdk@ping.com
Phone: (800) 746-4635
Fax: (404) 399-1670

Service: Pioneer Global
Access: Massachusetts
Contact: Craig Komins
E-mail: sales@pn.com
Phone: (617) 375-0200
Fax: (617) 375-0201

Service: Planet Access Networks
Access: New Jersey
Contact: Fred Laparo
E-mail: fred@planet.net
Phone: (201) 691-4704
Fax: (201) 691-7588

Service: PREPnet
Access: Pennsylvania
Contact: Thomas Bajzek
E-mail: twb+@andrew.cmu.edu
Phone: (412) 268-7870
Fax: (412) 268-7875

Service: Primenet
Access: Arizona
Contact: Clay Johnston
E-mail: info@primenet.com
Phone: (602) 870-1010 x109
Fax: (602) 870-1010

Service: PSCNET
Access: Eastern United States (PA, OH, WV)
Contact: Eugene Hastings
E-mail: pscnet-admin@psc.edu
Phone: (412) 268-4960
Fax: (412) 268-5832

Service: PSINet
Access: Nationwide
Contact: PSI, Inc.
E-mail: info@psi.com
Phone: (800) 82PSI82, (703) 620-6651

Fax: (703) 620-2430
Faxback: (800) 79FAX79

Service: QuakeNet
Access: California
Contact: Sales
E-mail: info@quake.net
Phone: (415) 655-6607

Service: The Rabbit Network, Inc.
Access: Michigan
Contact: Customer Liaison Services
E-mail: info@rabbit.net
Phone: (800) 456-0094
Fax: (810) 790-0156

Service: RAINet
Access: Oregon, SW Washington
Contact: Robert Chew
E-mail: info@rain.net
Phone: (503) 227-5665
Fax: (503) 297-9078

Service: Red River Net
Access: Minnesota, North and South Dakota
Contact: Craig Lien
E-mail: lien@rrnet.com
Phone: (701) 232-2227

Service: Rocky Mountain Internet, Inc.
Access: Colorado
Contact: Rich Mount
E-mail: mountr@rmii.com
Phone: (800) 900-RMII
Fax: (719) 576-0301

Service: Schunix
Access: Massachusetts
Contact: Robert Schultz
E-mail: info@schunix.com
Phone: (508) 853-0258
Fax: (508) 757-1645

Service: Scruz-Net
Access: California
Contact: Matthew Kaufman
E-mail: info@scruz.net

Phone: (800) 319-5555, (408) 457-5050
Fax: (408) 457-1020

Service: SeaNet
Access: Seattle
Contact: Igor Klimenko
E-mail: igor@seanet.com
Phone: (206) 343-7828
Fax: (206) 628-0722

Service: Sibylline, Inc.
Access: Arkansas
Contact: Dan Faules
E-mail: info@sibylline.com
Phone: (501) 521-4660
Fax: (501) 521-4659

Service: Sesquinet
Access: Texas
Contact: Farrell Gerbode
E-mail: farrell@rice.edu
Phone: (713) 527-4988
Fax: (713) 527-6099

Service: Sims, Inc. South
Access: Carolina
Contact: Jim Sims
E-mail: info@sims.net
Phone: (803) 762-4956
Fax: (803) 762-4956

Service: South Coast Computing Services
Access: Texas
Contact: Sales
E-mail: sales@sccsi.com
Phone: (800) 221-6478
Fax: (713) 917-5005

Service: SprintLink
Access: Nationwide
Contact: SprintLink
E-mail: info@sprintlink.net
Phone: (800) 817-7755
Fax: (703) 904-2680

Service: SURAnet
Access: Southeastern United States

Contact: Kimberly Donaldson
E-mail: kdonalds@sura.net
Phone: (301) 982-4600
Fax: (301) 982-4605

Service: Synergy Communications
Access: Nationwide
Contact: Jamie Saker
E-mail: jsaker@synergy.net
Phone: (402) 346-4638
Fax: (402) 346-0208

Service: Telerama Public Access
Access: Pennsylvania
Contact: Peter Berger
E-mail: sysop@telerama.lm.com
Phone: (412) 481-3505
Fax: (412) 481-8568

Service: THEnet
Access: Texas
Contact: Frank Sayre
E-mail: f.sayre@utexas.edu
Phone: (512) 471-2444
Fax: (512) 471-2449

Service: ThoughtPort, Inc.
Access: Nationwide
Contact: David Bartlett
E-mail: info@thoughtport.com
Phone: (314) 474-6870
Fax: (314) 474-4122

Service: UltraNet Communications, Inc.
Access: Massachusetts
Contact: Sales
E-mail: info@ultranet.com
Phone: (800) 763-8111, (508) 229-8400
Fax: (508) 229-2375

Service: US Net, Inc.
Access: Eastern United States
Contact: Services
E-mail: info@us.net
Phone: (301) 572-5926
Fax: (301) 572-5201

Service: VERnet
Access: Virginia
Contact: James Jokl
E-mail: net-info@ver.net
Phone: (804) 924-0616
Fax: (804) 982-4715

Service: ViaNet Communications
Access: California
Contact: Joe McGuckin
E-mail: info@via.net
Phone: (415) 903-2242
Fax: (415) 903-2241

Service: Vnet Internet Access, Inc.
Access: North Carolina
Contact: Sales (PHONE)
E-mail: info@vnet.net
Phone: (800) 377-3282
Fax: (704) 334-6880

Service: WestNet
Access: Western United States
Contact: Lillian or Chris
E-mail: staff@westnet.net
Phone: (914) 967-7816

Service: @ WiscNet
Access: Wisconsin
Contact: Tad Pinkerton
E-mail: tad@cs.wisc.edu
Phone: (608) 262-8874
Fax: (608) 262-4679

Service: WLN
Access: Washington
Contact: Rushton Brandis
E-mail: info@wln.com
Phone: (800) DIAL-WLN,
        (206) 923-4000
Fax: (206) 923-4009

Service: WorldWide Accesss
Access: Illinois
Contact: Kathleen Vrona
E-mail: support@wwa.com

Phone: (708) 367-1870
Fax: (708) 367-1872

Service: WVNET
Access: West Virginia
Contact: Harper Grimm
E-mail: cc011041@wvnvms.wvnet.edu
Phone: (304) 293-5192
Fax: (304) 293-5540

Service: XMission
Access: Utah
Contact: Support
E-mail: support@xmission.com
Phone: (801) 539-0852
Fax: (801) 539-0853

Storefront Developers

Developer: @sig.net
URL: http://www.sig.net

Developer: Access Market Square
URL: http://www.icw.com

Developer: The Alaskan Center
URL: http://alaskan.com

Developer: And Communications
URL: http://and.com

Developer: A Tangled Web
URL: http://www.cts.com/~atweb

Developer: Automatrix
URL: http://www.automatrix.com

Developer: Aztec Internet Services
URL: http://www.aztec.com/pub/aztec/
Phone: (410) 267-9467
E-mail: prpayne@aztec.com

Developer: Beverly Hills Software
URL: http://bhs.com/
469 South Bedford Drive
Beverly Hills, CA 90212
Phone: (310) 843-0414
Fax: (800) 230-8041

Developer: BizNet Technologies
URL: http://www.biznet.com.blacksburg.va.us

Developer: Branch Mall
URL: http://silkroute.com

Developer: Branch Mall
URL: http://branch.com

Developer: Byrd Polar Research Center
URL: http://www-bprc.mps.ohio-state.edu

Developer: CCL Internet Marketing Services
URL: http://cyber.cclims.com

Developer: C. G. Enterprises, Inc.
URL: http://usa.net/cge/cybergat.htm
PO Box 937
Guilderland, NY 12084-0937

Developer: Charm Net
URL: http://www.charm.net

Developer: Clark Net
URL: http://www.clark.net

Developer: Consumer Network Group
URL: http://www.msen.com/~niser/

Developer: Coolware
URL: http://none.coolware.com

Developer: CTS Network Services
URL: http://www.cts.com

Developer: Cyberbound Services
URL: http://indyunix.iupui.edu/~bdhornba/cybound.html
E-mail: bdh@cyberbound.com

Developer: CyberGate, Inc.
URL: http://www.gate.net

Developer: Cybermalls
URL: http://www.cybermalls.com

Developer: CyberPlex
URL: http://www.cyberplex.com

Developer: CyberWeb SoftWare
URL: http://www.charm.net/~web/CWSW.html
E-mail: CWSW@Stars.com

Developer: DeltaNet
URL: http://www.deltanet.com

Developer: Demon Internet
URL: http://www.demon.co.uk

Developer: DigiMark
URL: http://www.digimark.net

Developer: Digital Service Consultants, Inc.
URL: http://www.io.com/user/phoebus/dsc.html
3688 Clearview Avenue, Suite 211
Atlanta, GA 30340
Phone: (404) 455-9022
Fax: (404) 455-7714
E-mail: johnm@random9.randomc.com

Developer: Downtown Anywhere
URL: http://www.awa.com

Developer: Edge Creations Multimedia Production/Art Services
URL: http://offworld.wwa.com/edgeinfo.html
PO Box 693
Skokie, IL 60076-0693
Phone: (708) 675-9350
Fax: (708) 470-1515
E-mail: edgepres@wwa.com

Developer: ElectroMedia Interactive Web Design
URL: http://www.nets.com/electromedia
136 Piedra Loop
Los Alamos, NM 87504
Phone: (505) 470-2589, (505) 982-8383, ext. 20
E-mail: ElectroMedia@nets.com

Developer: eMall
URL: http://eMall.com

Developer: Entertainment Production Service, Inc.
URL:http://akebono.stanford.edu/yahoo/Business/Corporations/
Internet_Presence_Providers/Consulting/Entertainment_Production_
Service_Inc_/
E-mail: eps.com@ramp.com

Developer: Epublish
URL: http://www.fullfeed.com/epub/index.html
2806 Union Street
Madison, WI 53704
Phone: (608) 243-8000 V
E-mail: office@epublish.com

Developer: ESP Technologies
URL: http://gwis2.circ.gwu.edu/~powers/business.html
PO Box 8299
Bartlett, IL 60103-8299
Phone: (708) 931-1275
Fax: (708) 931-1275
E-mail: ESPairmail@aol.com

Developer: Evergreen Internet CyberMart
URL: http://cybermart.com

Developer: Flightpath Communications
URL: http://www.flightpath.com

Developer: FractalNet
URL: http://www.fractals.com

Developer: Frontier Internet
URL: http://www.frontier.net

Developer: Frontier Technology, Inc.
URL: http://www.greensboro.nc.us/frontier/
2007 Yanceyville Street
Greensboro, NC 27410
Phone: (910) 272-1274
E-mail: frontier@oasis.pdial.interpath.net

Developer: GetNet International FIESTA Web Server
URL: http://www.getnet.com

Developer: Global Electronic Marketing Service
URL: http://www.gems.com

Developer: Global Shopping Network
URL: http://www.gsn.com

Developer: Global X-Change
URL: http://www.globalx.net

Developer: Higgs America
URL: http://higgs.com/higgs.html
PO Box 3083
Van Nuys, CA 91407-3083
Phone: (818) 899-1875
Fax: (818) 890-0677
E-mail: sales@higgs.com

Developer: Hippermedia
URL: http://www.io.org/~farellc/hipper.html

219 Crawford Street
Toronto, Canada J6K 2V5
Phone: (416) 539-8057
Fax: (416) 539-0672
E-mail: farellc@io.org

Developer: Home Page Authoring
URL: http://www.iquest.net/cw/hpa/hpa.html
Phone: (317) 769-5049
Fax: (317) 769-6513
E-mail: dcook@iquest.net

Developer: Human Computer Interface
URL: http://holly.colostate.edu/~brauerjs/hci.html
E-mail: joshb@linden.fortnet.org

Developer: Hyper, Ink
URL: http://www.hyperink.com/hyperink
2039 Shattuck Avenue, Suite 206
Berkeley, CA 94704
Phone: (510) 286-7590
Fax: (510) 649-7130
E-mail: inquiry@hyperink.com

Developer: HyperNet
URL: http://wizard.pn.com/dbe/HyperNet/
E-mail: dbe@world.std.com

Developer: ImagePlaza, Inc.
URL: http://www.imageplaza.com/
Downtown Professional Building
314 Last Chance Gulch
Helena, MT 59601
Phone: (406) 443-7847
E-mail: assoc@imageplaza.com

Developer: I-MART
URL: http://www.wcci.com

Developer: InfiNet
URL: http://www.infi.net

Developer: InfoPlace—Internet Consulting Services
URL: http://www.infoplace.com/infoplace/
2276 Shelley Ave.
San Jose, CA 95124
Phone: (408) 371-1540
E-mail: zaveri@netcom.com

Developer: InfoPost
URL: http://www.infopost.com

Developer: InfoWest
URL: http://www.infowest.com

Developer: Ingress Communications
URL: http://tsw.ingress.com

Developer: Integra Software Corporation
URL: http://www.xmission.com/~americom/integra-credit.html
E-mail: rwk@integra.com

Developer: InterAccess
URL: http://www.interaccess.com

Developer: Inter-Active Yellow Pages [TM]
URL: http://netcenter.com

Developer: The Internet Access Channel
URL: http://www.tiac.net

Developer: The Internet Ad Emporium
URL: http://mmink.cts.com

Developer: Internet Design Group
URL: http://www.mall.net/
Phone: (415) 424-0747
E-mail: indigo@mall.net

Developer: Internet Information Mall
URL: http://marketplace.com

Developer: Internet Information Systems
URL: http://www.internet-is.com

Developer: Internet Media Services
URL: http://netmedia.com

Developer: Internet Presence & Publishing, Inc.
URL: http://www.ip.net

Developer: Internex Online
URL: http://www.io.org

Developer: InterWeb
URL: http://www.hickory.nc.us

Developer: Iquest Network Services
URL: http://www.iquest.com

Developer: Issue Dynamics, Inc.
Contact: Samuel A. Simon
URL: http://idi.net

901 15th Street, NW
Suite 230
Washington, DC 20005
Phone: (202) 408-1400
Fax: (202) 408-1134
E-mail: ssimon@idi.net

Developer: Knossopolis
URL: http://www.wimsey.com/~jmax/Knossopolis/
Phone: (604) 988-4770
E-mail: knossopolis@wimsey.com

Developer: Kudzu Creations
URL: http://www.america.net/com/kudzu/kudzu.html

Developer: Lucas Internet
URL: http://www.mbnet.mb.ca/lucas/
Phone: (204) 831-5122, (204) 992-2312
Fax: (204) 257-2259 F

Developer: Magellan Media Services
URL: http://www.webcom.com/~magellan

Developer: Magibox Incorporated
Contact: Louis Marcus
URL: http://www.magibox.net
1873 Hidden Oaks Drive
Germantown, TN 38138
Phone: (901) 757-7835
Fax: (901) 757-5875
E-mail: 1marcus@magibox.net

Developer: The Maloff Company
URL: gopher://marketplace.com/11/maloff

Developer: Marketing Communications/Editorial Services
Contact: Lee Philip Stral
URL: http://www.mcs.com/~leestral/home.html
Internet Consulting
608 W. Belmont Avenue
Chicago, IL 60657
Phone: (312) 929-5407
E-mail: leestral@mcs.com

Developer: Marsh-Birchal
URL: http://www.ios.com/~mb/
Phone: (609) 239-8023
E-mail: mb@ios.com

Developer: Matrix Marketplace
URL: http://www.internex.net

Developer: MediaCity
URL: http://www.MediaCity.com

Developer: MediaEdge: Consultants in New Media
URL: http://www.primenet.com/~laig/MediaEdge.dir/

Developer: Metaverse
URL: http://metaverse.com

Developer: MindSpring
URL: http://www.mindsprung.com

Developer: MountainNet Intefrated Services
URL: http://www.mountain.net

Developer: Multimedia Ink Designs
URL: http://mmink.com

Developer: NeoSoft
URL: http://www.neosoft.com

Developer: NetPress Communications
URL: http://www.netpress.com/
23 Mercy Street #1
Mountain View, CA 94041

Developer: Network Technology Corporation
URL: gopher://ftp.std.com/11/vendors/ntcorp

Developer: NetWorX, Inc.
URL: http://www.clark.net/pub/networx/networx.html
Phone: (410) 964-9684
E-mail: networx@clark.net

Developer: New South Showcase
URL: http://www.asa-net.com

Developer: Northcoast Internet
URL: http://www.northcoast.com

Developer: North Shore Access
URL: http://www.shore.net

Developer: Northwest Nexus
URL: http://www.halcyon.com

Developer: Novator
URL: http://www.novator.com

Developer: NPiX Interactive Web Marketing
URL: http://akebono.stanford.edu/yahoo/Business/Corporations/

Internet_Presence_Providers/Consulting/NPiX_Interactive_
Web_Marketing/
Phone: (404) 892-1971
Fax: (404) 892-1971
E-mail: info@npixi.com

Developer: Office Techniques Information Services
URL: http://www.otisnet.com/otis
E-mail: otis@otisnet.com

Developer: Online Marketspace
URL: http://www.omix.com

Developer: OnRamp
URL: http://www.ramp.com

Developer: OnRamp Online
URL: http://www.onramp.net

Developer: Orange Distribution, Inc.
URL: http://akebono.stanford.edu/yahoo/Business/Corporations/
Communications_and_Media_Services/Graphic_Design/Orange_
Distribution__Inc_/
E-mail: yahoo@akebono.stanford.edu

Developer: Oslonett
URL: http://www.oslonett.no

Developer: Peek & Associates, Inc.
URL: http://www.teleport.com/~peekpa/
5765 SW 161st Avenue
Beaverton, OR 97007-4019
Phone: (503) 642-2727
Fax: (503) 642-0961
E-mail: benpeek@AOL.com

Developer: PICnet of Dallas/Ft. Worth
URL: http://www.pic.net

Developer: Primenet
URL: http://www.primenet.com

Developer: Professional Computer Consultants
Contact: Jim Hepburn
3226 Benda Street
Los Angeles, CA 90068-1506
Fax: (213) 874-9282
E-mail: hepburn@primenet.com

Developer: Public.com
URL: http://www.public.com

Developer: RFW Associated Enterprises
Contact: Robert F. Wojczyk
6 Monska Drive
East Hampton, MA 01027-2716
Phone: (413) 529-0811
Fax: (413) 529-0811
E-mail: rob.wojczyk@the-spa.com

Developer: Roi Co., Ltd.
Contact: Hans Shimizu Karlsson, Director
6-27-1-107 Shinjuku, Shinjuku-ku
Tokyo, Japan, 160
Phone: +83-3-5286-7636
Fax: +81-3-3208-2901
E-mail: hanske@roi.twics.com

Developer: Shopping2000
URL: http://www.shopping2000.com

Developer: Simon Edgett Computer Services
URL: http://smailbox.island.net/secs.html

Developer: South Coast Computing Services
URL: http://www.sccsi.com

Developer: The Sphere Information Services
URL: http://www.thesphere.com

Developer: SpiderWeb.com
URL: http://www.spiderweb.com

Developer: SRVnet, Inc.
URL: http://www.srv.net

Developer: StudioX
URL: http://www.nets.com

Developer: Tag Online Mall
URL: http://www.tagsys.com

Developer: Technoware (Germany)
URL: http://eietu2.et.tu-dresden.de/iet/technoe.htm
E-mail: jordan@eietu2.et.tu-dresden,de

Developer: Tecnation Digital World
URL: http://www.tecnation.com/tecnation/
555 Bryant Street #257
Palo Alto, CA 94301
Phone: (415) 327-4332
Fax: (415) 327-1910
E-mail: hello@tecnation.com

Developer: Tela
URL: http://www.winternet.com/~tela/
1024 Wedgwood Lane South
Eagan, MI 55123
Phone: (612) 452-0162 V
Fax: (612) 588-4218
E-mail: tela@winternet.com

Developer: Teleport
URL: http://www.teleport.com

Developer: TelTECH Computer Consulting
URL: http://bb.iu.net/teltech/
Palm Beach, FL
Phone: (407) 455-4809
E-mail: teltech@iu.net

Developer: Thunderstone Software - EPI
URL: http://www.thunderstone.com
11115 Edgewater Drive
Cleveland, OH 44102
Phone: (216) 631-8544 V
Fax: (216) 281-0828 F
E-mail: info@thunderstone.com

Developer: Traveller Information Services
URL: http://www.traveller.com

Developer: TriNet Services
URL: http://www.trinet.com

Developer: UltraNet Communications, Inc.
URL: http://www.ultranet.com

Developer: UniPress W3 Services Division
URL: http://www.unipress.com/w3/
UniPress Software, Inc.
2025 Lincoln Highway
Edison, NJ 08817
Phone: (800) 222-0550, ext. 920
Fax: (908) 287-2100

Developer: Utah Wired
URL: http://www.utw.com

Developer: Virtumall
URL: http://virtumall.com

Developer: Walter Shelby Group Web Services
URL: http://www.shelby.com/pub/wsg/html/web/home.html
4618 Maple Avenue
Bethesda, MD 20814
Phone: (301) 718-7840
E-mail: web@shelby.com

Developer: The Web Lab
URL: http://www.dircon.co.uk/web-lab/index.html
E-mail: helpdesk@dircon.co.uk

Developer: WebLink
URL: http://www-bprc.mps.ohio-state.edu/
cgi-bin/hpp?rich_weblink.html

Developer: Webscope
URL: http://www.webscope.com

Developer: Webvertiser
URL: http://www.sccsi.com/welcome.html
Phone: (713) 326-4886
E-mail: whitney@sccsi.com

Developer: Wimsey
URL: http://www.wimsey.com

Developer: WorldWide Access
URL: http://sashimi.wwa.com

Developer: World-Wide Collectors Digest
URL: http://www.wwcd.com

Developer: Xmission
URL: http://www.xmission.com

Developer: Xynergy
URL: http://www.nets.com/xynergy.html
ElectroMedia Interactive Web Design
135 Piedra Loop
Los Alamos, NM 87504
Phone: (505) 470-2589 V
Fax: (505) 982-8383, ext. 20
E-mail: ElectroMedia@nets.com

10
Cybermalls

Cybermalls are the electronic equivalent of our modern day shopping centers commonly found in communities throughout the world. Cybermalls are World Wide Web locations on the Internet. Just as for years merchants have set up shop in traditional shopping malls, electronic storefront owners are finding that participation in cybermalls can raise the number of visitors that stop by and shop. See Fig. 10-1.

Cybermalls come in all sizes. While there are no rules governing how malls must be designed, there seem to be two common groups:

❏ *Actual storefronts:* This type of mall contains several storefronts (sometimes similar in nature, other times not) that have gathered together to open up shop in a common or covenient location. The number of storefronts can range from only a few to hundreds. When you arrive at this kind of mall, the data for the various storefronts is contained on the same computer system.

❏ *Signposts:* This kind of mall does not contain actual storefronts. Rather, it displays information about various storefronts with Hypertext Links to enable visitors (once they've found the storefront that can suit their needs) to immediately jump to the actual location of the storefront, wherever it may be on the Internet.

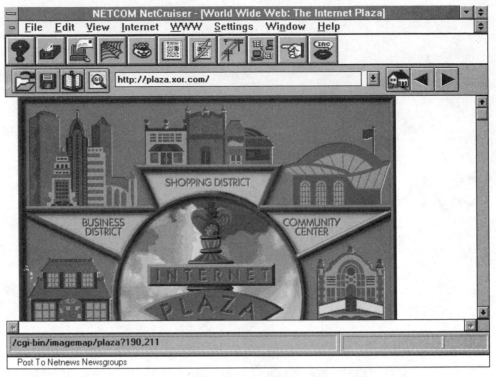

Figure 10-1.   A cybermall called Internet Plaza.

Typically, mall visitors will be unable to determine whether they are visiting an actual mall or a signpost mall. Fortunately, understanding the difference is irrelevant, because you can get to your desired storefront location using either kind of mall.

Surfing from cybermall to cybermall is quickly becoming a common practice by individuals wishing to find a certain kind of storefront. Considering the limitations imposed on commercial storefront owners by the Internet community itself, cybermalls have become a major means by which they can advertise their business. As a future storefront owner yourself, you should seriously consider opening your business within a storefront and/or advertising your storefront on a number of signpost malls.

Most cybermall owners charge a fee to open a storefront within their community or to advertise a business in their storefront listings.

Most cybermalls also provide programming services to assist storefront owners in the development of their storefront. If you're in the market for storefront developers, this chapter can provide you with many options.

New cybermalls are popping up daily, and some older ones disappear just as quickly. However, in a recent search of the Internet, the authors were able to identify the following cybermalls. It would be wise to visit a number of malls to determine which one you might be interested in join-ing or using to advertise your new storefront. For the following cyber-malls, the mall name and URL address are provided. Use the NetCruiser software and the Web browser function to visit any mall you wish. Re-member to type in the URL address exactly as you see it—upper and lower case is important.

If, when attempting to visit a mall, you receive an error message, it often means the computer system supporting the distant mall may be down for repairs or maintenance. If you should encounter this situation, try again at a later date. If you continue to receive the same error message, that mall may have gone out of business.

How can you determine which mall may be right for you? Since malls vary in the number and kind of storefronts that participate, you should set aside a few hours and surf the Net. Visit as many malls as you can and de-termine which malls:

❑ Have the best overall appearance.

❑ Provide storefront owners with good visability (i.e., storefronts are not hard to find, buried deep in several layers of menu systems).

❑ Contain storefronts that might attract the same kind of customers you hope to attract.

❑ Are attracting large numbers of visitors already.

Of the following cybermalls, those in **bold** lettering are exceptionally attractive and warrant your review.

A-TRA Shopping Centres
http://www.achilles.net/~atra/atrahpge.html

Above & Beyond—The Tall & All Mall
http://199.170.0.46/

Access Market Square
http://www.icw.com/ams.html

Bay Area Shopping Guide
http://netmedia.com/ims/shopping/ba_shopping_center_guide.html

BizNet Shopping Center
http://www.bnt.com/shopping.html

Blacksburg Electronic Village Mall
http://www.bev.net/mall/index.html

Branch Information Services
http://www.branch.com/

Catalog Central
http://catalog.florida.com/cchome.htm

CommerceNet
http://www.commerce.net

Crystal Portal
http://cybersight.com/cportal/cphome.html

CyberMall
http://www.nstn.ca/cybermall/first.html

CyberMont
http://www.cybermalls.com/cymont/cymonmal.htm

CyberSales
http://www.cts.com/catalog/

Cyteria Village
http://cyteria.netaxs.com/

Deep Space Mall
http://www.deepspace.com/deepspace.html

DigiCash Cybershop
http://www.digicash.com/digishop/shopmain.html

Downtown Anywhere
http://www.awa.com/index.html

ElectraCity
http://inforamp.net/electracity/index.html

eMall
http://eMall.Com/Home.html

Eureka! The Web Junction
http://www.wilder.com/eureka.html

Financial Mall@(2)
http://akebono.stanford.edu/yahoo/Business/Corporations/
Financial_Services/Financial_Mall/

First Virtual's Infohaus
http://www.infohaus.fv.com/

Florida Internet Commerce Center
http://www.florida.com/

Glass Wings Arcade
http://www.aus.xanadu.com/GlassWings/arcade.html

IMALL
http://akebono.stanford.edu/yahoo/Business/Corporations/
Internet_Presence_Providers/IMALL/

IndustryNET@(3
http://akebono.stanford.edu/yahoo/Business/Corporations/
Manufacturing/IndustryNET/

INFOMART - Dallas, Texas
http://www.onramp.net/infomart/infomart.html

Infoplus
http://www.infop.com/index.html

Internet Business Connection
http://www.charm.net/~ibc/

Internet Center for Arts and Crafts Gift Shop
http://www.xmission.com/~arts/

Internet Express
http://usa.net

Internet Media Services Marketplace
http://199.171.168.11/ims/market/market.html

Internet Presence and Publishing
http://www.ip.net

Internet Shopkeeper
http://www.shopkeeper.com/shops/

Internet Shopping Mall
http://isms.com/

Internet Shopping Network
http://www.internet.net/

Internet Traders
http://www.tecfen.com/itraders/

MarketBase(tm) Online Catalog
http://galaxy.einet.net/hytelnet/FEE062.html

MarketPlace.com
http://marketplace.com/

Mexplaza
http://mexplaza.udg.mx

Net-Mart
http://netmart.com/

NetMall(tm)
http://www.ais.net/netmall/

NetMarket - The Market
http://www.netmarket.com/netmarket/bin/market/:grm|:mode=text

Onramp Access
http://www.onr.com/

One World Plaza
http://www.wincorp.com/windata/OneWorldPlaza/
OneWorldPlaza.html

Openmarket.Com
http://www.openmarket.com

PICnet E-Mall
http://www.pic.net/lobby/lobby.html

PIXINET's Hawaii's Market Place
http://www.pixi.com/hawaii_marketplace.html

Rocky Mountain Cyber Mall
http://www.csn.net/malls/rmcm/

Sell-it on the WWW
http://www.xmission.com/~wwwads/

Shopping2000
http://www.shopping2000.com

Shopping IN
http://www.onramp.net/shopping_in/

Stanford Shopping Center (2)
http://akebono.stanford.edu/yahoo/business/Corporations/
Shopping_Centers/Stanford_Shopping_Center/

Super Mall
http://www.supermall.com/

TAG Online Mall
http://www.tagsys.com/

Tarheel Mall
http://netmar.com/mall/

The Internet Access Co.
http://www/tiac.net/

The Internet Plaza
http://xor.com/

The WebStore
http://www.webstore.com/

The World Square
http://www.w2.com/

Village Potpourri Mall
http://www.vpm.com/

Virtual Mall
http://www.virtualmall.com/

Virtual Mirror Business Directory
http://mirror.wwa.com/mirror/busdir/busdir.htm

WebMall - Digital's Electronic Mall
http://www.service.digital.com/html/emall.html

World Wide Mall
http://www.olworld.com/olworld/
WorldWide Marketplace
http://www.cygnus.nb.ca/

Starting Access Market Square has been one of the most exciting things I've ever done. The idea to market on the Internet actually came from some of my cohorts. The idea of the mall was
a joint decision. In any case, it's been a thrill a minute.

The startup costs for the mall were expensive, the ongoing costs are ex-
orbitant, but it's been very rewarding and exciting. I've talked with people
throughout the world, although most of my discussions have been with people in the United States. Everyone is interested in the Internet, but especially
from the aspect of someone who's out doing something with it. And there
are some interesting people out there doing things with and on the Internet.

I've stayed awake many nights throughout the last year wondering if
this was going to work. Will people actually want to put their products in
my mall? Will they want to stay there? Will they make enough money to
make it all worth while? Will anyone on the Internet ever start buying? Can
I stay innovative enough to attract people into my mall?

So here I am nearly a year later with many of the same questions con-
suming both my waking and sleeping hours. Is it worth it? That question
deserves a resounding "YES!" The problems will continue, people are still
not buying much on the Internet, but everyone with whom I speak and put
in my mall has the same positive attitude. Things will work, and they are
starting to pick up some now. People on the Internet will become accus-
tomed to seeing us die-hards with our shopping centers sticking through
both the good times and bad. Working with the store owners has been
great, and I can say I've talked with many great people throughout the United States and the world. It's been worth every dime and sleepless night.

Mark Tolman
President, InterConnect West
The Developers of Access Market Square
1-801-487-0888
http://www.icw.com/ams.html

11
Netiquette Guide

by Arlene H. Rinaldi

Like any other highway, especially those still under construction, the Internet can best be experienced if we all follow a few basic rules or guidelines regarding our behavior. In a civilized society, either in real space or cyberspace, rules governing our behavior are necessary if we are all to enjoy a safe and comfortable ride.

The Internet is relatively new, growing rapidly, and creating experiences and situations we have never known before. Such a situation can be ripe for abuse by individuals more concerned about their personal desires than the enjoyment of all. While there are no laws governing behavior that can be enforced by a legal court of law, there are accepted behavior guidelines, and failure to comply can result in punishment by the Internet community.

The guidelines for behavior found within this chapter, as prepared by Arlene H. Rinaldi, Senior Computer Programmer/Analyst at Florida Atlantic University, a lady who knows her way around the Net, can increase your enjoyment and success as a new member of the Internet community. They can also help you avoid the punishments that will be imposed on you if you fail to understand the rules of the road.

As a new Internet traveler, some of the terms and rules presented in this chapter may be unfamiliar. That's OK! As you continue to learn more about using the Internet and its various functions, return often to this chapter and review the suggested rules of behavior associated with the functions you wish to use.

Background

The Internet is rapidly developing its own unique culture formed by a diverse group of people of various religions, nationalities, genders, and experiences. The Internet, commonly referred to as cyberspace, is a worldwide melting pot of opinions and ideas. The people using the resources on the Internet have been known to call themselves "netizens" (network citizens), which makes them part of a whole new social and cultural evolution—a new community of people. They are adventurers on an electronic frontier, where their individual voices can change and shape the future of electronic communications as we know it. Terms used frequently in exploring and discovering cyberspace are "mining," "surfing," and "driving the information superhighway." The Internet is a place where worldwide information and communication are constantly expanding and evolving. Just as with any culture, there are customs that provide guidelines and cohesiveness to the people involved.

When I first started working on the Internet in 1990, there were fewer people interfacing with the Internet and, of course, fewer resources. Originally, there was an unspoken "agreement" among users to act and respond in a certain way while working on the Internet. If this agreement was broken, the user could expect to be "flamed" (a Net term meaning to receive an argumentative or belligerent response via e-mail) or possibly even lose Internet access depending on how flagrantly the "rules" had been abused. The rules have not changed even though resources are greater now and the people coming online are more diverse and understandably unfamiliar with nebulous conventions.

When I first started working with e-mail and Usenet several years ago, I made simple but honest "mistakes" and was thoroughly chastised for them, either in the form of teasing or irate e-mail messages. Just a few of my "simple" mistakes were:

❏ Typing mail messages all in upper case (typically considered SHOUTING!).

❏ Sending a subscription notice for an online discussion group directly to the list instead of to the List Serv handling electronic addition/deletion of members.

  Over 1000 people received my personal e-mail message that I wanted to subscribe to the discussion group. I received a great deal of irate e-mail on that mistake. (Subscription details are sent to the List Serv. Only messages meant to be read by the entire group should go to the list.)

❏ Sending a personal e-mail message to a Usenet group that I thought would go only to the original poster of the message, who lived locally.

It was in the form of "Let's meet for lunch and talk about this." Well, I received quite a few teasing mail messages as to whether I would "buy" for everyone reading that particular Usenet Newsgroup. (Same issue: Personal messages should go to the individual's e-mail address, not the entire list.)

I began to investigate whether there were any online guides that would assist in putting an end to my "newbie" approach towards working with electronic communication. At that same time several people on the Internet began to define guidelines by which to assist users in communicating via an electronic medium that did not allow for a great deal of personal or graphical creativity. The method for creating electronic e-mail messages does not allow any of the "bells and whistles" that standard word processing software packages make available in formal letter writing. The universal format for an e-mail message is ASCII or, as it is commonly known now, plain vanilla ASCII. If users want to highlight text when sending e-mail, they cannot use underline, bold, or italics to make a specific point. Other punctuation mark standards needed to be invented to globally symbolize a point.

Most of the guidelines I uncovered online were specific to Usenet or e-mail, but none answered questions on the multiple resources available on the Internet. When I provided Internet training to the faculty and staff at Florida Atlantic University (FAU), I decided to help those taking my courses by creating guidelines using my own experiences and using other online documents geared towards network etiquette. I also created guidelines for the different resources available on the Internet, i.e., FTP, Telnet, List Serv. I wanted the document to be simple, to the point, and not overly excessive in do's and don'ts. Moreover, because of the ever changing face of the Internet, I also wanted the document to be easy to change as Cyberspace itself changed and grew.

I asked for help in the form of suggestions and comments from the members of an online discussion group called NETTRAIN. The members of NETTRAIN are mainly worldwide Internet trainers who are tasked as I am to train others at their various institutions or organizations on the Internet resources.

With the NETTRAIN member suggestions and comments, my own experiences and from other online documents, I developed and now maintain the document "The Net: User Guidelines and Netiquette." The document's original application was for internal university use. As a result of this document being available online in various formats, it has been referenced worldwide in newsletters, journals, training programs, and quoted in books.

The guidelines are not to be misconceived as laws; nor are they rules that detract from the concept of free expression on the Internet. Rather the guidelines are meant to provide helpful hints on some common and frequently addressed questions or global "standards." The guidelines assist users of the Internet to know what is considered abuse of available resources, and they help users to be responsible in accessing or transmitting information through the Internet.

Each organization on the Internet should provide and inform its users on expected standards of conduct when using its network and when accessing other networks while using Internet resources. The punitive measures for not adhering to the organization's policies should also be provided. Those using the Internet are held accountable for abuses against their organizational policies for acceptable network use and by Internet infractions against their local, state, national, or international laws.

If users are irresponsible or discourteous to others or if they abuse the resources that allow them and others to share information and communicate, they take the risk of the Internet community using its own form of chastisement against them. The community will use their individual or collective voices to educate, inform, and sometimes even ostracize by way of flame messages or by contacting the users' Network Administrator of flagrant abuses. Acting responsibly and following general customs allows users to experience a global adventure of open communication, information, and resources, which ultimately provides a unique exploration of the electronic frontier called cyberspace.

The Net: User Guidelines and Netiquette

Introduction

Users of the network must recognize their responsibility in having access to vast services, sites, systems, and people. Users are ultimately responsible for their actions in accessing network services.

The Net is not a single network; rather, it is a group of thousands of individual networks that allow traffic to pass among them. The traffic sent out to the Internet may actually traverse several different networks before it reaches its destination. Therefore, users involved in this internetworking must be aware of the load placed on other participating networks.

As a user of the network, you may be allowed to access other networks (and/or the computer systems attached to those networks). Each network or system has its own set of policies and procedures. Actions that are routinely allowed on one network or system may be controlled, or even forbidden, on other networks. Users must abide by the policies and procedures of other networks and systems. The fact that users *can* perform an action does not imply that they *should*.

The use of the network is a privilege, not a right, which may temporarily be revoked at any time for abusive conduct. Such conduct would include:

❏ The placing of unlawful information on a system.

❏ The use of abusive or otherwise objectionable language in either public or private messages.

❏ The sending of messages that are likely to result in the loss of recipients' work or systems.

❏ The sending of chain letters or broadcast messages to lists or individuals.

❏ Any other type of use that would cause congestion of the networks or otherwise interfere with the work of others.

Permanent revocations can result from disciplinary actions taken by a panel judiciary board called on to investigate network abuses.

E-mail User Responsibility

The content and maintenance of a user's electronic mailbox is the user's responsibility:

❏ Check e-mail daily and remain within your limited disk quota.

❏ Delete unwanted messages immediately since they take up disk storage.

❏ Keep messages remaining in your electronic mailbox to a minimum. E-mail messages can be downloaded or extracted to files then to disks for future reference.

❏ Never assume that your e-mail can be read by no one except yourself; others may be able to read or access your e-mail.

❏ Never send or keep anything that you would not mind seeing on the evening news.

File User Responsibility

The content and maintenance of a user's disk storage area is the user's responsibility:

❏ Keep files to a minimum. Files should be downloaded to your personal computer's hard drive or to disks.

❏ Routinely and frequently virus-scan your system, especially when receiving or downloading files from other systems to prevent the spread of a virus.

❏ Your files may be accessible by persons with system privileges; so do not maintain anything private in your disk storage area.

Telnet Protocol

❏ Many telnetable services have documentation files available online (or via file transfer protocol). Download and review instructions locally, as opposed to tying up ports trying to figure out the system.

❏ Be courteous to other users wishing to seek information, or the institution might revoke Telnet access. Remain only on the system long enough to get your information; then exit off the system.

❏ Screen-captured data or information should be downloaded to your personal computer's hard disk or to disks.

Anonymous File Transfer Protocol

❏ Users should respond to the Password prompt with their e-mail address, so that, if that site chooses, it can track the level of FTP usage. If your e-mail address causes an error, enter Guest for the next Password prompt.

❏ When possible limit downloads, especially large downloads (one megabyte or more), after normal business hours locally and for the remote FTP host, preferably late in the evening.

❏ Adhere to time restrictions as requested by archive sites. Think in terms of the current time at the site that's being visited, not of local time.

❏ Copy downloaded files to your personal computer hard drive or disks to remain within disk quota.

❏ When possible, inquiries to Archie (a search program used to locate anonymous FTP files) should be in e-mail form.

❏ When downloading programs, check for copyright or licensing agreements. If the program is beneficial to your use, pay any author's registration fee. If there is any doubt, don't copy it. There have been many occasions on which copyrighted software has found its way into FTP archives. Support for any downloaded programs should be requested from the originator of the application. Remove unwanted programs from your systems.

Electronic Communications

❏ For e-mail, List Serv groups, Mailing Lists, and Usenet, keep paragraphs and messages short and to the point.

❑ Focus on one subject per message, and always include a pertinent subject title for the message. That way the user can locate the message quickly.

❑ Don't use the academic networks for commercial or proprietary work.

❑ Include your signature at the bottom of e-mail messages. Your signature footer should include your name, employment position and affiliation, and Internet and/or Bitnet addresses and should not exceed more than four lines. Optional information could include your address and phone number.

❑ Capitalize words only to highlight an important point or to distinguish a title or heading. *Asterisks* surrounding a word also can be used to make a stronger point. Capitalizing whole words that are not titles is generally regarded as SHOUTING!

❑ Limit line length and avoid control characters.

❑ Follow chain of command procedures for corresponding with superiors. For example, don't send a complaint via e-mail directly to the "top" just because you can.

❑ Be professional and careful what you say about others. E-mail is easily forwarded.

❑ Cite all quotes, references, and sources and respect copyright and license agreements.

❑ It is considered extremely rude to forward personal e-mail to mailing lists or Usenet without the original author's permission.

❑ Be careful when using sarcasm and humor. Without face-to-face communications, your joke may be viewed as criticism.

❑ Acronyms can be used to abbreviate when possible, however messages that are filled with acronyms can be confusing and annoying to the reader. Examples:

    IMHO = in my humble/honest opinion

    FYI = for your information

    BTW = by the way

    Flame = antagonistic criticism

    :-) = happy face for humor

    :-(= sad face for sadness

List Serv, Mailing Lists, Discussion Groups

Some mailing lists have low rates of traffic; others can flood your mailbox with several hundred e-mail messages per day. Numerous incoming messages, from various list servers or mailing lists by multiple users, require extensive system processing, which can tie up valuable resources.

❑ Subscription to interest groups or discussion lists should be kept to a minimum and should not exceed what your disk quota can handle—or you for that matter.

❑ When you join a list, monitor the messages for a few days to get a feel for what common questions are asked and what topics are deemed off limits. This is commonly referred to as *lurking*. When you feel comfortable with the group, then start posting.

❑ See if there is a *FAQ* (frequently asked questions) for a group that you are interested in joining. Veteran members get annoyed when they see the same questions every few weeks or at the start of each semester.

❑ Follow any and all guidelines that the list owner has posted; list owners establish the local netiquette standards for their lists.

❑ Keep in mind that some discussion lists or Usenet groups have members from many countries. Don't assume that they will understand a reference to TV, movies, pop culture, or current events in your country. If you must use the reference, please explain it.

❑ Don't join a list just to post inflammatory messages (mail bombing). This upsets most system administrators and you could lose access to the net.

❑ Keep your questions and comments relevant to the focus of the discussion group.

❑ If another person posts a comment or question that is off the subject, do *not* reply to the list and keep the off-subject conversation going publicly.

❑ When someone posts an off-subject note, and someone else criticizes that posting, you should *not* submit a gratuitous note saying, "Well, I liked it and lots of people probably did as well, and you guys ought to lighten up and not tell us to stick to the subject."

❑ When going away for more than a week, unsubscribe or suspend mail from any mailing lists or List Serv services.

❑ If you can respond to someone else's question, do so through e-mail. Twenty people answering the same question on a large list can fill your mailbox (and those of everyone else on the list) quickly.

❑ When quoting another person, edit out whatever isn't directly applicable to your reply. Don't let your mailing or Usenet software automatically quote the entire body of messages you are replying to when it's not necessary. Take the time to edit any quotations down to the minimum necessary to provide context for your reply. Nobody likes reading a long message in quotes for the third or fourth time, only to be followed by a one-line response: "Yeah, me too."

❏ Use discretion when forwarding a long e-mail message to group addresses or distribution lists. It's preferable to reference the source of a document and provide instructions on how to obtain a copy. If you must post a long message, warn the readers with a statement at the top of the mail message. Example: WARNING: LONG MESSAGE

❏ If you crosspost messages to multiple groups, include the name of the groups at the top of the e-mail message with an apology for any duplication.

❏ Resist the temptation to flame others on the list. Remember that these discussions are *public* and meant for constructive exchanges. Treat the others on the list as you would want them to treat you.

❏ When posting a question to the discussion group, request that responses be directed to you personally. Post a summary or answer to your question to the group.

❏ When replying to a message posted to a discussion group, check the address to be certain it's going to the intended location (person or group). It can be very embarrassing if they reply incorrectly and post a personal message to the entire discussion group that was intended for an individual.

❏ When signing up for a group, save your subscription confirmation letter for reference. That way if you go on vacation you will have the subscription address for suspending e-mail.

❏ Use your own personal e-mail account; don't subscribe using a shared office account.

❏ Occasionally subscribers to the list who are not familiar with proper netiquette will submit requests to Subscribe or Unsubscribe directly to the list itself. Be tolerant of this activity, and possibly provide some useful advice as opposed to being critical.

❏ Other people on the list are not interested in your desire to be added or deleted. Any requests regarding administrative tasks such as being added or removed from a list should be made to the appropriate area, not the list itself. E-mail for these types of requests should be sent to the following respectively:

LISTSERV GROUPS- LISTSERV@host

MAILING LISTS - listname-REQUEST@host or listname-OWNER@host

For either Mailing Lists or List Serv groups, to subscribe or unsubscribe, in the body of the message include:

SUBSCRIBE listname <your first name>, <your last name>
(To be added to the subscription) or

UNSUBSCRIBE listname
(To be removed from the subscription)

World Wide Web (WWW)

❑ Do not include very large graphic images in your hypertext markup language (HTML) documents. It is preferable to have postage-sized images that the user can click on to enlarge a picture. Some users with access to the Web are viewing documents using slow modems and downloading these images can take a great deal of time.

❑ When including video or voice files, include next to the description a file size, i.e., (10 KB or 2 MB), so that users know how long it will take to download the file.

❑ Keep naming standards for URLs simple and concise with changes in case. Some users do not realize that sites are case-sensitive or they receive URLs verbally where case sensitivity is not easily recognizable.

❑ When in doubt about a URL, try accessing the domain address first, then navigate through the site to locate the specific URL. Most URLs begin with the node address of WWW followed by the site address.

Examples:

http://www.cern.ch
http://www.fau.edu
http://www.ibm.com
http://www.cpsr.org

❑ A URL that includes only an image map and no text might not be accessible to users that do not have access to a graphical Web browser. Always include the option of text links in your URL documents.

❑ URL authors should always protect their additions to the Web by including trademark (™) or copyright (©) symbols in their HTML documents.

❑ URL authors should include an e-mail address at the bottom (or in the address area) of all HTML documents. Because of the nature of HTML links, users can automatically link to your HTML document and have questions about it, but will not know whom to contact if the e-mail address is not available.

❏ URL authors should always include a date of last revision, so that users linking to the site can know how up-to-date the information has been maintained.

❏ Infringement of copyright laws, obscene, harassing or threatening materials on Web sites can be in violation of local, state, national or international laws and can be subject to litigation by the appropriate law enforcement agency. Authors of HTML documents will ultimately be responsible for what they allow users worldwide to access.

The Ten Commandments for Computer Ethics from the Computer Ethics Institute

1. Thou shall not use a computer to harm other people.
2. Thou shall not interfere with other people's computer work.
3. Thou shall not snoop around in other people's files.
4. Thou shall not use a computer to steal.
5. Thou shall not use a computer to bear false witness.
6. Thou shall not use or copy software for which you have not paid.
7. Thou shall not use other people's computer resources without authorization.
8. Thou shall not appropriate other people's intellectual output.
9. Thou shall think about the social consequences of the program you write.
10. Thou shall use a computer in ways that show consideration and respect.

Appendixes

A
Internet Glossary

Acceptable use policy (AUP)   Rules that describe the kinds of activities that are allowed on a certain computer network.

Account   The right to use a particular computer network or access to a computer on the Internet. A right that may be purchased or obtained for free from the owner of the network or access service. Accounts are registered under your name, and are usually protected by the use of a secret password.

Address   A unique coding system used on the Internet to identify you from all the other users, for such purposes as sending and receiving e-mail.

Anonymous FTP   A function that enables computer files to be shared among members of the Internet community without requiring the person who is requesting to download a file from a remote computer to identify him or herself to the owner of the remote computer system.

Archie   A search program used to locate anonymous FTP files on the Internet. Once you have located a file using Archie, you may then use anonymous FTP to retrieve it to your computer system.

Archive   Storing files on a host computer for retrieval at some future time, or compressing files using a compression program such as PKZip, to reduce the size of the files to allow for more files to be saved on a computer system.

ARPAnet   The network developed and funded by the Department of Defense that was the predecessor to today's Internet.

Article   A message that someone may post to a Newsgroup, which is then readable by anyone who requests updates to the same Newsgroup.

AT&T Mail   A commercial electronic e-mail system that allows individuals to exchange messages via the Internet.

Baud   The rate at which computer modems can transfer data from one location to another, usually expressed as bits per second (bps). Common baud rates include 2400, 9600, 14,400 and 28,800 bps.

Binary file   A computer file usually containing data, other than text (ASCII) information. Usually contains executable program code (code that actually runs a software program).

Bit   The smallest amount of information that can be stored by a computer.

BIX   A commercial computer network service.

Bounce   What occurs when an e-mail message is returned to the sender because of an insufficient address.

Bulletin board system (BBS)   A computer system that enables individuals to "call in" using a communications program and a modem to gain access to and/or exchange information and files. Bulletin board systems usually focus on a particular subject or topic of interest, and may be used by an individual, organization, or business as a medium of information exchange.

Byte   A means of expressing the size of a particular computer file or program. One byte is equal to eight bits of information.

Cello   A graphical program (PC Windows format) for use in accessing the World Wide Web. The Cello program was written at Cornell Law School. Mosaic is a similar program.

Chameleon   A commercial program that can be used with Windows to connect to the Internet via a serial line Internet protocol (SLIP) connection.

Chat   "Talking," keyboard to keyboard, with other individuals on a computer network in real time (as it is occurring). Internet Relay Chat (IRC) is used to accomplish this task on the Internet.

Client   The program used to access a remote server on a distant network and to the devices, programs, and files controlled by the server.

Cyberspace   A term coined by William Gibson in his novel *Neuromancer,* meaning a place without any physical location, such as the Internet or, more specifically, an electronic storefront.

Downloading   Electronically transferring files from a remote computer to your own computer.

Dumb terminal   Basically just a computer monitor and a keyboard. Dumb terminals rely on other computers for their computing power. When you use your computer to dial up another computer, your computer becomes a dumb terminal for the distant computer.

E-mail   The abbreviation for electronic mail, an electronic system whereby you may send and receive messages and files to other people with access to the same e-mail service as you.

E-mail address   The electronic address that signifies your location on a computer network service, a location from which you may send and receive messages and files.

Eudora A program that allows for the exchange of e-mail messages.

Fax modem A computer device that can send and receive fax messages and data files.

File transfer protocol (FTP) A system designed to transfer files on the Internet from one computer to another. Several common dial-up protocols include xmodem, ymodem, zmodem, and kermit.

Finger A command that allows a user on one computer to retrieve information from a remote computer system.

Flame A strongly worded e-mail message that often contains a controversial opinion or criticism directed at another person.

Flame wars Situations where groups of people send flame e-mail messages to other individuals, usually in response to a previous e-mail message.

Frequently asked questions (FAQ) A list of questions (and answers) that are often asked about a particular topic that is accessible to individuals who themselves wish to learn more about the topic.

FTP-by-mail A system whereby you may obtain files from a remote computer by return e-mail, rather than by FTP. You first send a request for a particular file to a server and then shortly afterwards receive the file information as a regular e-mail message.

Gateway A machine that connects two or more networks and routes information from one network to the other. *See also* Mail gateway.

Gopher A system allowing you to search the Internet for specific information. Gopher displays the found information in a hierarchical form similar to a table of contents.

Hacker A computer programmer or higher-level computer user who attempts to gain unauthorized access via a computer network to restricted information and sites.

Home page The first page (or screen) that you encounter when you visit an electronic storefront on the World Wide Web.

Host A computer on the Internet that makes available files and other information to individuals who wish to access such information.

Hypertext (Hypertext Links) A means of linking information found in one text document with related information found elsewhere in the same document or in another document. Hypertext enables readers to follow a string or common thread of knowledge as predetermined by the author.

Hypertext markup language (HTML) A program used to create documents for use with World Wide Web locations (i.e., electronic storefronts).

Internet Relay Chat (IRC) A system that allows two computer users, linked by a network, to communicate keyboard to keyboard in real time.

Jughead A program similar to Veronica that allows an individual to search the Internet for specific information.

Kermit A means of transferring files electronically; developed at Columbia University.

List Serv   An automatic mailing system used on the Internet that enables you to request and receive information via e-mail on a particular topic or interest of your choice.

Local area network (LAN)   A collection of computers (usually not extending more than a few miles in diameter) linked together by phone lines or cables for the purpose of sharing information.

Logging off   Disconnecting from a remote computer or network service.

Logging on   Gaining access to a remote computer or computer network service, often requiring you to indicate your name and a password.

Lurking   "Listening in" to a Newsgroup discussion, Mailing List, or online forum without actually participating in or contributing to the topic at hand.

Mail exploder   A system whereby a message is sent via e-mail to every individual on a list who has requested the information.

Mail gateway   A machine that connects two or more electronic e-mail systems (that may be dissimilar and on different networks), and transfers e-mail messages between the systems.

Mailing list   A list of individuals (which you may join) who wish to receive, via e-mail, regular updates of information on a subject or topic of interest.

Mosaic   A graphical program to access the World Wide Web, including storefronts. Copies of Mosaic are available for downloading from the Internet free of charge.

National Science Foundation Network (NSFNET)   A network sponsored by the U.S. government for the exchange of scientific research information.

Netiquette   A set of guidelines outlining the behavior considered socially acceptable on the Internet.

Network   A group of computers connected for the purpose of sharing information.

Newsgroup   A system whereby you may electronically post messages about a specific topic for viewing and response by others on the Internet. Thousands of Newsgroups exist covering topics of all kinds.

Newsreader   A program that allows you to read Newsgroups that you have requested and received, and to post responses if you wish.

Node   A device or computer that is attached to a network.

Online   Being connected (logged on) to a computer network service, such as America Online, CompuServe, PRODIGY, or the Internet.

Packet   A small chunk of information. On the Internet, the sending computer breaks every transmission of text or data into packets, which then travel independently around the network to the intended receiving computer. A packet is the smallest unit of information transmitted on the Internet. Packets are reassembled by the receiving computer into the original file or data.

Page   A unit of organization of information on the World Wide Web. Information that is accessible via the Web (such as electronic storefronts) is organized and displayed as pages. A page may contain text, graphics, sound, and other elements.

Protocol   An agreed-on set of procedures used to exchange information from one computer to another.

Router   A machine that determines the best route by which information can be sent from one computer network to another.

Serial line Internet protocol (SLIP)   A special method of transferring data between two dissimilar computer network systems, such as when a personal computer is connected to a computer directly wired into the Internet.

Server   A program running on a computer network that enables individuals with the proper authorization to access various devices (printers, hard drives, etc.) and programs and files located somewhere on the network.

Shareware   Software that may be obtained free of charge or at a minimal cost for testing. If you wish to keep the program, you are required to forward a fee to the author of the program. Most of the software available for downloading from the Internet is shareware.

Snail mail   A term used to describe first class mail delivery offered by the United States Postal Service, since it is always slower than electronic e-mail.

Special interest group (SIG)   A group of individuals who share a common interest in a particular topic.

Telnet   A protocol and utility that enables you to log onto other computers on the Internet and actually control the function of the remote computer.

Transmission control protocol/Internet protocol (TCP/IP)   This combination of network protocols and transport level protocols allows for computers on the Internet or other networks to speak the same language for the purpose of transmitting information. TCP is the protocol that handles connections; and IP is a lower-level protocol that handles packets of information. These two protocols, working together, make sure that data on the Internet arrives at its desired location.

Uploading   Electronically transferring files from your computer to a remote computer.

Usenet   A worldwide system dedicated to the dissemination of information made available on the Internet by the Newsgroup service.

User ID   The name assigned to or selected by you for gaining access to a computer network service or a specific location on the Internet.

Veronica   A search program, similar to Archie, that searches the Gopher system menus to help you find information.

WAIS (wide area information server)   A program that is used to index large text files stored on servers. WAIS can be used to find and retrieve database documents based on words that are defined by the person conducting the search.

Web browser   A program that enables World Wide Web locations (including electronic storefronts) to be viewed in a graphical, multimedia presentation style, often combining words, graphics, animation, video, and sound.

Wide area network (WAN)   A collection of interconnected computers that may span hundreds or even thousands of miles.

World Wide Web (the Web or WWW)   A series of thousands of documents found on the Internet, interconnected using a system of linked (hypertext) words, allowing an Internet traveler to jump from one document to another in an unending process.

Xmodem   A set of standards for the electronic transfer of files over a network. Computers equipped with xmodem software have the ability to check the receiving data to ensure it was not corrupted during transmission, and to request the sending computer to resubmit corrupted data if necessary.

Ymodem   Similar to xmodem, but faster.

Zmodem   Similar to both xmodem and ymodem, but faster than both.

B
Storefront Planning Worksheet

Use this worksheet (which starts on the next page) to record your thoughts and plans as you begin to design your electronic storefront. Consider this worksheet as your preliminary "to do ..." list, a central depository of your ideas, concerns, questions, preferences, and objectives.

Depending on your storefront objectives, some of the following information may be irrelevant. Don't be concerned if you are unable to provide information for all categories, even for most categories. You are not expected to do so. Much of this information may not be known until you've had time to discuss your basic ideas with a storefront developer. For now, just put your basic ideas in writing.

The information recorded here should be shared with your storefront developer to enable him or her to "see" your vision, and to act as a guide in creating your storefront.

Feel free to photocopy this worksheet. Use additional sheets of paper if more writing space is needed.

Storefront development team members include:

❏ Team leader: _____

❏ Storefront developer: _____

   Options: _____

   _____

   _____

   _____

   Final choice: _____

❏ Graphic artist(s): _____

   Options: _____

   _____

   _____

   _____

   Final choice: _____

❏ Internet access service provider: _____

   Options: _____

   _____

   _____

   _____

   Final choice: _____

❏ Informational researchers: _____

   Options: _____

   _____

   _____

   _____

   Final choice: _____

❏ Clerical support: _____

   Options: _____

   _____

   _____

   _____

   Final choice: _____

❏ Other team members: _____

_____

_____

_____

Purchase a compression program:

❏ PKZip (PC)
❏ Stuffit (Macintosh)
❏ Other

Check references on the following team members:

Name: _____   ❏ Reference OK

Name: _____   ❏ Reference OK

Name: _____   ❏ Reference OK

Name: _____   ❏ Reference OK

Name: _____   ❏ Reference OK

Secure signed letters of agreement with the following team members:

With: _____   ❏ Agreement secured

With: _____   ❏ Agreement secured

With: _____   ❏ Agreement secured

With: _____   ❏ Agreement secured

With: _____   ❏ Agreement secured

Learn how to use NetCruiser software program:

	Completed
Install software.	❏
Register account with NetCom.	❏
Establish e-mail address.	❏
Send first e-mail message.	❏
Access Mailing Lists.	❏
Access Usenet Newsgroups.	❏
Telnet to a distant computer.	❏
Download an FTP file.	❏
Search the Net using Gopher.	❏
Access storefronts via the Web.	❏
Chat with someone online with IRC.	❏

Design elements: The following design elements will be used in my storefront (indicate information where necessary):

☑ Home page

❏ Additional Pages (approximately # _____)

❏ Banner (describe appearance): _____

_____

_____

❏ Title of storefront: _____

❏ URL address: _____

❏ Subtitle of storefront: _____

❏ Items on the Main menu: _____

_____

_____

_____

_____

❏ Items on the first submenu: _____

_____

_____

_____

_____

_____

❏ Items on the second submenu: _____

_____

_____

_____

_____

_____

❏ Items on the third submenu: _____

_____

_____

_____

_____

_____

❏ Items on the fourth submenu: _____

_____

_____

_____

_____

_____

❏ Items on the fifth submenu: _____

_____

_____

_____

_____

_____

❏ Items on the sixth submenu: _____

_____

_____

_____

_____

_____

❏ Items on the seventh submenu: _____

_____

_____

_____

_____

_____

❏ Items on the eighth submenu: _____

_____

_____

_____

_____

_____

❏ Items on the ninth submenu: _____

_____

_____

_____

_____

_____

❏ Items on the tenth submenu: _____

_____

_____

_____

_____

_____

❏ Customer service information link. Information to be displayed:

_____

_____

_____

_____

_____

❏ Location and purpose of Help links:

_____

_____

_____

_____

_____

❑ Location of Hypertext Links. Link following words/phrases to:

Word/Phrase   Link to

_____   _____

_____   _____

_____   _____

_____   _____

_____   _____

❑ General overall content of the text information to appear on each page:

Page 1 _____

Page 2 _____

Page 3 _____

Page 4 _____

Page 5 _____

Page 6 _____

Page 7 _____

Page 8 _____

Page 9 _____

Page 10 _____

Additional pages _____

❑ Graphics to be incorporated: _____

_____

_____

❑ Downloadable files to be incorporated: _____

_____

_____

❑ Searchable databases to be incorporated: _____

_____

_____

❑ Order form(s) to be incorporated: _____

_____

_____

❏ Install credit card authorization? ❏ Yes   ❏ No   ❏ Uncertain

❏ Offer a text only display option? ❏ Yes   ❏ No

❏ Offer a foreign language display option? ❏ Yes   ❏ No

   If yes, which language(s)? _____

   _____

❏ Animation sequences to be incorporated? (*Caution:* Requires long download times!)

   _____

   _____

   _____

❏ Photographs to be incorporated? _____

   _____

   _____

   _____

❏ Video clips to be incorporated? (*Caution:* Requires long download times!)

   _____

   _____

   _____

❏ Sound clips to be incorporated? (*Caution:* Requires long download times!)

   _____

   _____

   _____

❏ Links to other storefronts:

   _____

   _____

   _____

❏ Cybermalls to contact regarding advertising:

   _____

   _____

   _____

❏ Computer equipment that needs to be purchased:

_____

_____

_____

❏ Products to be sold from storefront:

_____

_____

_____

_____

❏ Services to be sold from storefront:

_____

_____

_____

_____

❏ Target customers:

_____

_____

_____

_____

❏ Advertising options on the Internet:

_____

_____

_____

_____

❑ Advertising options off the Internet:

_____

_____

_____

_____

_____

❑ Option(s) for customers to obtain additional information:

_____

_____

_____

_____

❑ Ordering options:

_____

_____

_____

_____

❑ Shipping and handling procedures:

_____

_____

_____

_____

❑ Person(s) responsible for managing orders:

_____

_____

_____

_____

❏ Text information to be compiled by (names of individuals):

_____

_____

_____

_____

_____

❏ Work on storefront scheduled to begin (date) _____

❏ Storefront scheduled to go live on Internet (date) _____

❏ Breakdown of costs:

_____

_____

_____

_____

_____

_____

_____

Total anticipated costs = $ _____

❏ Person(s) responsible for day-to-day management of storefront:

_____

❏ Person(s) responsible for evaluation of storefront:

_____

❏ Criteria for determining success of storefront:

_____

_____

_____

_____

_____

_____

❏ Other Items:

_____

_____

_____

_____

_____

_____

_____

_____

_____

_____

_____

_____

_____

_____

_____

_____

_____

_____

_____

_____

_____

_____

C

Internet Resource Directory

This chapter contains a listing of resources that can enhance your general enjoyment and use of the Internet, and in particular your ability to conduct business through your electronic storefront. Information is divided into six categories:

❏ Books
❏ Magazines
❏ Newsletters
❏ Software programs (Internet access)
❏ Software programs (HTML editors)
❏ Video tapes

Books

The following books may be obtained at most bookstores and libraries. Listings are presented in the following order: title, author, publisher, and cost.

Access the Internet, Peal (Sybex, $19.99).

Business Users Guide to the Internet, Dern (Prentice Hall, $29.95).

Canadian Internet Handbook, Carroll (Prentice Hall, $16.95).

The Complete Idiot's Next Step, Kent (Alpha Books, $19.95).

The Complete Idiot's Pocket Resource, Goldman (Alpha Books, $9.95).

The Complete Idiot's Guide to the Internet, Kent (Alpha Books, $19.95).

The Complete Internet Directory, Braun (Fawcett Books, $25.00).

Connecting to the Internet, Estrada (O'Reilly Publishing, $15.95).

Directory of Directories on the Internet, Newby (Meckler, $29.50).

Doing More Business on the Internet, Cronin (Vans, $29.95).

Easy Internet, Miller (Que, $24.99).

The Easy Internet Handbook, Mostafa (Hi Will, $20.00).

Every Student's Guide to the Internet, Pitter (MGWH, $15.75).

Everybody's Guide to the Internet, Gaffin (MITP, $14.95).

Exploring the Internet, Malamud (Prentice Hall, $26.95).

Field Guide to the Internet, Microsoft Press (Microsoft Press, $9.95).

Finding It on the Internet, Gilster (Wiley, $19.95).

Get on the Internet in 5 Minutes, Hayden Development (Hayden, $9.95).

Guerilla Marketing on the Internet, Levinson (Houghton-Mifflin, $12.70).

Guided Tour of the Internet, Crumlish (Sybex, $19.99).

Global Advantage on the Internet, *Cronin (Vans, $29.95).*

Handbook of the Internet, *Strangelove (Van Nostrand, $ Not Available).*

Hands-On Internet, *Sachs (Prentice Hall, $29.95).*

Hitchhiker's Guide to the Electronic Highway, *Kane (MIS, $21.95).*

HTML for Fun and Profit, *Mary E. S. Morris (Prentice Hall, $35.95).*

How the Internet Works, *Eddings (Ziff-Davis, $24.95).*

How to Grow Your Business on the Internet, *Emery (IDG, $24.95).*

How to Make a Fortune on the Internet, *Canter (Harper, $20.00).*

How to Use the Internet, *Butler (Ziff-Davis, $17.95).*

Information Superhighway, *Que Development (Que, $19.99).*

Instant Internet Access Multimedia, *Jamsa (Jamsa, $49.95).*

Instant Internet Guide, *Heslop (Addison, $14.95).*

Internet, *Marine (Prentice Hall, $28.00).*

Internet 101, *Glossbrenner (T A B B, $19.95).*

Internet Access Essentials, *Tittel (Academic, $24.95).*

Internet Anywhere, *Gardner (Prentice Hall, $29.95).*

Internet Basics, *Lambert (Random, $27.00).*

Internet Book, *Comer (Prentice Hall, $24.95).*

Internet Business Book, *Ellsworth (Wiley, $22.95)*.

Internet Business Companion, *Angell (Addison, $19.95)*.

Internet Business Guide, *Resnick (Sams, $24.95)*.

Internet Business Handbook, *Dern (Prentice Hall, $29.95)*.

Internet Companion, *Laquey (Addison, $12.95)*.

Internet Connection, *Quarterman (Addison, $32.25)*.

Internet Dictionary, *Hayden Development (Hayden, $12.95)*

Internet for Dummies Quick Reference, *Levine (IDG, $8.95)*.

Internet for Dummies, *Levine (IDG, $19.95)*.

Internet for Dummies Starter Kit, *Levine (IDG, $34.99)*.

Internet for Everyone, *Wiggins (McGraw-Hill, $45.00)*.

The Internet from A to Z, *Crumlish (Sybex, $16.99)*.

Internet Help Desk for Dummies, *Kaufeld (IDG, $16.99)*.

Internet Navigator, *Gilster (Wiley, $24.95)*.

Internet Roadmap, *Falk (Sybex, $14.99)*.

Internet Starter Kit for Windows, *Engst (Hayden, $30.00)*.

Internet Simplified, *Maran (IDG, $19.99)*.

Internet Unleashed, *Bang (Sams, $39.95)*.

The Internet via World-Wide Web, *Bowne (Ziff-Davis, $29.95)*.

Internet White Pages, *Godin (IDG, $29.95)*.

Internet Yellow Pages, *Hahn (Osborne, $27.95)*.

Making Money on the Internet, *Glossbrenner (T A B B, $19.95)*.

Marketing on the Internet, *Ellsworth (Wiley, $24.95)*.

Marketing on the Internet, *Lamb (Orei, $19.95)*.

Marketing on the Internet, *Mathiesen (Maximum, $34.95)*.

Minding Your Cybermanners on the Internet, *Rose (Alpha, $12.99)*.

More Internet for Dummies, *Levine (IDG, $19.95)*.

Mosaic Access to the Internet, *Tauber (Sybex, $19.99)*.

Mosaic for Internet for Dummies, *IDG Staff (IDG, $19.99)*.

Mosaic, *Gunn (Sams, $25.00)*.

Multimedia and Hypertext, *Nielsen (Academic, $29.95)*.

Navigating the Internet, *Smith (Sams, $24.95)*.

New Riders' Official Internet, *Maxwell (New Riders', $29.95)*.

On Internet Ninety-five *(Meckler, $34.95)*.

PC Internet Tour Guide, *Fraase (Ventana, $24.95)*.

Pocket Guides to the Internet (6 titles), *Veljok (Meckler, $9.95 each)*.

Riding the Internet Highway, *Fisher (New Riders, $16.95)*.

Shopping on the Internet, *Easton (IDG, $19.99)*.

Spinning the World Wide Web, *Ford (Vans, $29.95)*.

Success with Internet, *Jamsa (Jamsa, $29.95)*.

Teach Yourself the Internet, *Randall (Sams, $25.00)*.

Ten Minute Guide to the Internet, *Kent (Alpha Books, $12.95)*.

Tricks of the Internet Gurus, *Sams Staff (Sams, $39.95)*.

What's on the Internet?, *Gagnon (Peachpits, $24.95)*.

The Whole Internet User's Guide, *Krol (O'Reilly, $24.95)*.

Windows Internet Tour Guide, *Fraase (Ventana, $24.95)*.

Your Internet Consultant, *Savetz (Sams, $25.00)*.

Zen and the Art of the Internet, *Kehoe (Prentice Hall, $23.95)*.

Magazines

These magazines may be obtained at most bookstores and magazine stands.

Internet World (Meckler Publications, $4.95/copy).

NetGuide (CMP Publications, $2.95/copy).

Online Access (Online Access Publications, $4.95/copy).

Newsletters

The following newsletters may be ordered by contacting the publisher directly by phone or e-mail. A URL address is provided if the publisher also maintains a Web location on the Internet.

Internet Business Advantage
(Wentworth Publishing, $67/year).
Phone: (800) 638-1639

InterNet Success
(Williams Publishing, $21/year).
Phone: (216) 848-4591
URL: http://icw.com/america/amerway/success.html

Digital Future
(Hart Publishing, $52/year).
Voice/Fax: (303) 987-3246
E-mail: jhart@teal.csn.net

Software Programs (Internet Access)

Some type of Internet software program is necessary when connecting your computer to the Internet. *Note:* The copy of NetCruiser bundled with this book will provide you with full Internet access.

A variety of additional options are available for both Windows and Macintosh computers from the following list. Programs may be purchased by contacting the publisher or from a local computer software dealer. In certain cases, additional information may be obtained via e-mail or by visiting the publisher's URL location.

Instant InterRamp
A full access to the Internet software package
PSI
Phone: (800) PSI-0852

Internet Chameleon
An Internet connectivity software
Net Manage
Phone (408) 973-7171
E-mail: sales@netmanage.com

Internet Express
A full access to the Internet software package
Phoenix Technologies
Phone: (800) 452-0120

Internet in a Box
A full access to the Internet software package
SPRY
E-mail: IBOXINFO29@SPRY.COM

Internet Starter Kit
Internet access software
Que Software

Internet Works
Internet access software
Brooklink Technologies
Phone (800) 453-SURF

NetCruiser
A full access to the Internet software package
NETCOM
Phone: (800) 501-8649
E-mail: info@netcom.com

Superhighway Access
A full access to the Internet software package
Frontier Technologies
Phone: (800) 929-3054

Super Mosaic
A full access to the Internet software package
Phone: (800) 500-4411

TCP / Connect II
An Internet access software
InterCon
Phone: (800) NET2YOU
URL: ftp.intercon.com

WinPac and WinPac Complete
Windows-based graphical interface to Internet
NOTIS Systems, Inc.

Software Programs (HTML Editors)

These software programs are designed to help you produce hypertext markup language (HTML) documents, otherwise known as hypertext documents. Additional information may be obtained by contacting the publisher directly. Additional HTML editors are available on the Internet. To view a list of ones you may download, travel to the following URL address:

> http://union.ncsa.uiuc.edu/HyperNews/get/www/html/
> editors.html

Storefront developers often make such editors available to storefront owners who wish to assist in the creation of hypertext documents. Ask your storefront developer for more information.

Internet Assistant
Microsoft Press
Phone: (800) 426-9400
Format: Word for Windows

Wordperfect Internet Publisher
Novell
Phone: (800) 451-5151
Format: Windows

Video Tapes

Introduction to the Internet
70 minutes
Digital Data Express
San Jose, CA
Phone: (800) 335-LEARN
$49.95

The Information Superhighway: Understanding and Using the Internet
30 minutes
FreeRange Media
Phone: (800) 327-4225
E-mail: info@freerange.com
$29.95

D

Installing and Using NetCruiser

Welcome to the Internet!

In just a few minutes, you'll be cruising the Internet using NetCruiser from Netcom, one of the best Internet access services and software programs available on the market today!

NetCruiser is an easy-to-use Windows-based program that allows you to point and click your way around the Internet. Netcom provides you with both user-friendly software and an access phone number to fully access all that the Internet has to offer. Your computer actually becomes part of the Internet!

With NetCruiser, you can:

❏ *Send electronic mail* (e-mail) to individuals who have access to the Internet, including all the popular commercial online services, such as America Online, Apple eWorld, CompuServe, and PRODIGY.

❏ *Access Usenet Newsgroups,* a worldwide bulletin board with over 9500 categories of interesting information. You can read, post, and download articles on any topic you can imagine.

❏ *Cruise the World Wide Web (WWW),* the most exciting, graphical area of the Internet and check out electronic storefronts all around the world.

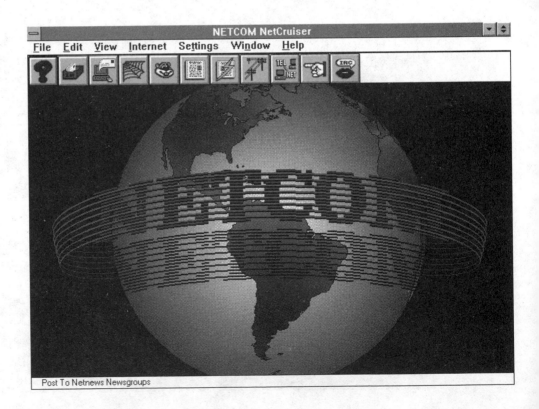

❏ *Use Gopher* to search for and retrieve information stored on computers worldwide.

❏ *Use File Transfer Protocol (FTP)* to upload and download files (text, audio, video, graphics, etc.) from your computer to remote computers worldwide.

❏ *Access Telnet*, to log onto other computers anywhere around the world from your computer keyboard.

❏ *With IRC*, chat keyboard to keyboard with individuals worldwide.

❏ And much, much more!

System Requirements

To operate NetCruiser for Windows you'll need a 386 or faster IBM PC-compatible system running MS-DOS 5.0 or greater and Microsoft Windows 3.1 or Windows 95. You should have 4 megabytes of RAM (8 megabytes of RAM if you're running Windows 95) and at least 4 megabytes of free hard disk space. You'll also need a 14.4-baud or faster modem; a 28.8-baud modem is highly recommended.

Billing Charges

Access to the Internet via Netcom is very economical. During the installation procedure, you will be asked to enter a credit card number. Netcom is available for the following fee:

Monthly flat fee = $19.95

Registration fee = $25.00
Note: This fee has been waived by Netcom to all readers of *Selling on the Internet.*

At the $19.95 monthly rate, you will be given 40 free hours of connect time to the Internet each month—anytime, day or night. Your Netcom service also includes free access to the Internet anytime Saturday and Sunday and during the hours from midnight to 9 a.m. (local time). If you use more than the 40 free hours (very unlikely), each additional hour of connect time will be charged at the rate of $2.00 per hour.

There is no charge for your copy of NetCruiser enclosed in *Selling on the Internet,* and future upgrades are available for downloading from Netcom at no charge. You will be notified when you log onto the Netcom service when upgrades are available.

Technical Support

Once installed, use the Help menu in NetCruiser to learn more about how to use the program. If you experience any problems that cannot be solved with the use of the online Help program, please call Netcom Technical Support at (408) 983-5970.

Installing NetCruiser

For Windows 3.1:

❏ Insert the enclosed 3.5-in. diskette into drive A: or B:

❏ From the Windows Program Manager File Menu, choose Run

❏ Enter A:\Setup or B:\Setup (as appropriate to your system) into the Run dialog box

❏ In the Welcome to NetCruiser Setup dialog box, choose a directory for installation (default is C:\netcom). Wait for all files to be copied to your hard drive.

❏ Choose the type of modem you have installed, the baud rate at which you wish to communicate, and a COM port for your modem.

❏ Select a NETCOM telephone number closest to your location.

For Windows 95:

❏ Click on the Start button.

❏ Select the Settings option.

❏ Select the Control Panel option.

❏ Double click on the Add/Remove Programs option.

❏ Click on the Install button.

❏ Insert the enclosed disk into your 3.5-in. drive

❏ (If necessary) Change the default install path from a:\install to b:\install.

❏ Click on the Finish button.

❏ In the Welcome to NetCruiser Setup dialog box, choose a directory for installation (default is C:\netcom). Wait for all files to be copied to your hard drive.

❏ (If requested) Choose the type of modem you have installed, the baud rate at which you wish to communicate, and a COM port for your modem.

❏ Select a NETCOM telephone number closest to your location.

❏ Click on the OK button.

The installation program will create in Windows 3.1 a new program group or in Windows 95 a new program item called NETCOM containing:

1. NetCruiser launch icon.
2. NetCruiser Help icon.
3. NetCruiser Registration icon.
4. NetCruiser Getting Started Help icon.
5. NetCruiser Upgrade Program icon.

Note: The Help and Getting Started Help programs are provided separately, so that you may use them without having to log onto the Netcom service.

Registering with NetCruiser

Before you begin to use NetCruiser to access the Internet, you must register your copy of the software program with Netcom. To do this:

❑ From the NETCOM program group or item, select the NetCruiser Registration icon.

❑ Click OK in the Welcome to NetCruiser dialog box. Fill in the Registration Information form. If a registration code is printed on your diskette label, be sure to enter the code when prompted to do so. If not, click Continue on the Registration Code dialog box.

❑ Enter a user name and password.

❑ Fill in the appropriate boxes for your modem to reach the Netcom toll-free registration number (i.e., a telephone number prefix of 9 to reach an outside line and whether or not your phone service provider requires a 1 before the 800 area code). Then click OK.

❑ At this point, please supply the requested credit card information.

The NetCruiser Registration procedure will provide diagnostic information if the process fails. If you wish, the Change Input button allows you to edit your information. At completion you will be asked to select a local access number, as new numbers may have been loaded into the Directory during the registration procedure.

Connecting with NetCruiser

❑ From the NETCOM program group or item, select the NetCruiser icon.

NetCruiser will display several status messages across the top of the dialog box in the center of your display to advise you as to the status of the

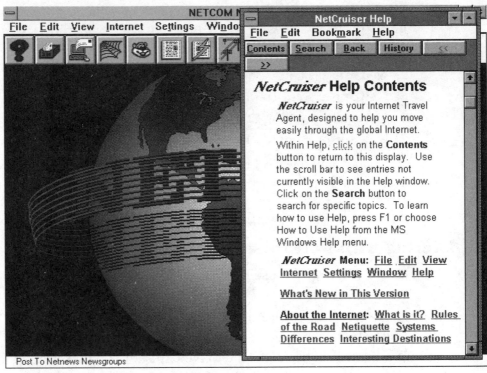

NetCruiser Help system.

log-on procedure. Also, the latest information from Netcom will appear once connection is made. After reading the information, click on OK to clear the screen and display the main NetCruiser screen.

Using the NetCruiser software program

NetCruiser is equipped with an extensive Help system to quickly and easily assist you in learning all about the many functions and features contained within the program. No printed user's manual is necessary. To learn how to use any of the NetCruiser functions, select the menu items Contents from the Help menu, and then select the function you wish to learn more about.

Index

About the Authors

James C. Gonyea of Gonyea & Associates, Inc. and Wayne M. Gonyea of Online Solutions, Inc. have for years operated profitable storefront businesses on the Internet and various commercial online services. Wayne Gonyea specializes in creating Internet storefront operations for entrepreneurs. James Gonyea is the founder and director of America Online's Career Center, one of his storefront locations that won him national recognition as "America's guru of electronic career planning and placement." James Gonyea has authored several books on career planning and doing business on the Internet, including *The Online Job Search Companion* and, with Wayne as a co-author, *Electronic Resumes* (both by McGraw-Hill). Readers wishing to contact the authors may do so at:

James Gonyea
President and CEO
Gonyea & Associates, Inc.
1151 Maravista Drive
New Port Richey, Florida 34655
813-372-1333
Email: Careerdoc@aol.com
Internet Storefront:
Internet Career Connection (http://iccweb.com)

Wayne Gonyea
President
Online Solutions, Inc.
1584 Rt 22B
Morrisonville, NY 12962
518-643-2873
Email: online@ns.cencom.net
Internet Storefront:
Made in America Mini-Mall!
(http://amsquare.com/america/made.html)
Internet Storefront:
Career and Resume Management for the 21st Century
(http://crm21.com)